PSYCHIC
EMPATH ABILITIES

*A Survival Guide to Overcome Stress and Negative
Energy. How High Sensitive People Can Increase
Intuition, Clairvoyance, Telepathy and Aura
Reading To Open Their Third Eye*

WILLOW KUMAR

TABLE OF CONTENTS

INTRODUCTION

Are you the kind of person that is very sensitive and emotional? Do you pay close attention to your emotional sphere and the energies around you? Do you want to understand yourself better and the world around you? Whether you are a casual fan of psychic phenomena or you have a burning desire to develop your psychic abilities, this book has the thing that you need. I am sure you are struggling with handling your emotional problems and you are trying to find help in understanding your current situation and want to get guidance on how you can improve it. Well, look no further because after reading this book, you will be more informed about the world of psychics and that will help you on how you can face your problems and solve them.

Drop whatever it is you are doing and let us dive into the world of Psychic Empaths and their psychic abilities. Psychics are people with an awakened extrasensory perception that can perceive the information from the universe that is hidden from our normal senses. This involves the positive and negative auras or energy that is coming from everything including animals, places, and us humans. Psychics also have supernatural abilities which include telepathy, clairvoyant healing, aura reading, and an open third eye that helps us do those things and more, which you will learn how to do after you finish this book. Psychics are more vulnerable to negative energies because they can sense them more than an average person. That is why you will also learn how to protect yourself from all the negative energy that is found in your surroundings and how to cultivate and preserve the positive energy in yourself. This book will also help you be happier and live a positive life, you will also learn how to be yourself and how to take care of yourself. We will also cover what psychic empaths are, and find out if you are one of them. And if you are wondering if your dreams have meaning, this book also has information about dream interpretations to help you find out what is the meaning behind the dreams you are having.

After reading this book, you will see that you have acquired the knowledge on how to handle your life better. You will also be introduced to the world of spirit guides which will help you and give you guidance whenever you need it. All of your misconceptions about psychics will also be clarified. So, what are you waiting for? Continue reading to find out how you can develop your sleeping psychic abilities and be presented with the wonders of the world of auras and energy.

CHAPTER 1: INTRODUCTION TO INCREASING YOUR PSYCHIC EMPATH ABILITIES

How to Develop Your Psychic Abilities

Psychics are people with an activated extrasensory perception that allows them to perceive the world in a more detailed manner because they can see the hidden information about our universe that is not perceived by our normal senses. Psychics can also develop supernatural abilities that allow them to do things that other people cannot, like the communication of thoughts using only the power of their mind and without the use of any physical interactions.

Every person in the world has innate psychic abilities, some people just have more developed psychic abilities because they are used to using their psychic abilities while others are not even aware that they have it or just simply do not believe in it. Having more developed psychic abilities could help you understand the world better and help you have an improved life. Psychics see the world differently than a normal person because they understand the things that a normal person is not even aware of.

If you want to improve your psychic abilities, you need to pour some of your time and attention into practicing it just like any other skill. Developing your psychic abilities is a long and slow process but by following these tips you can improve your psychic abilities development at a much more comfortable and faster pace.

Believe In Yourself

The very first step to developing your psychic abilities starts within you. Psychic abilities come from within us. As I said before, everyone has innate psychic abilities that reside deep within us and we just need a little help to develop them and make them come out naturally. Believing in yourself should be your first goal because if you do not believe that you have psychic abilities it will not manifest. Remove all the doubts that you have in you and believe in the power of the universe that is given to us. After believing in yourself, everything that you think will become a possibility, that is the power of our mind because what you project to the universe is also what the universe will project back to you. Our mind is a strong tool that makes our reality what it is.

Eliminate Negativity

While psychic abilities are born with us, what cultivates it is the positivity that emanates from you and the universe. Eliminating negativity from you and your environment will help reduce the negative energies surrounding you that hinder the development of your psychic abilities. These negativities can come from a bad environment that you stay in or a person that is doing something that can make you feel negative emotions such as anger and sadness. Being around negative people can also affect you because psychics can absorb the negative energy of the people around them. Keeping your house clean can help you remove negativity from your home and spending less time or cutting ties completely with the person that gives you negativity can be hard but once you do it will definitely improve your life and help you achieve your goal and develop your psychic abilities.

Flower Visualization

This will be the first exercise that you will do to actually start developing psychic ability. You need to get a flower and put it in front of you, then you have to focus on it and look at every detail on the flower that is in front of you. After taking a good look at the flower, you have to close your eyes and focus, then try to think about the flower that is in front of you. Picture it in your mind as clear as you can and with as many correct details as you possibly can. After doing the previous steps as best as you can, open your eyes and try to examine the flower that is in front of you, check whether you get the details of the flower in your mind's eye correctly. Repeat the exercise and try to get the results to be as close to the original object as possible.

Flower visualization helps you develop a clear psychic vision. At first, the picture in your mind might be a bit blurry and not specific but after some practice, you can visualize the flower perfectly and you can try to do it with different objects later on. This exercise will help you capture more specific and detailed pictures in your mind's eye and it will also help you in communicating with your spirit guide. It is recommended to repeat this exercise a few times a week.

Communicate With Your Spirit Guide

After developing a clear psychic vision, you can now start to communicate with your spirit guide for them to assist you in your psychic ability development journey. You can start communicating with your spirit guide by simply acknowledging that they are there and asking your spiritual guide out loud or in your mind to show themselves to you. You can ask your spirit guide to show you a picture in your mind to help you develop your clairvoyance ability even further.

However, most of the time your spirit guide is already communicating with you without you even being aware of it. One example could be your spirit guide sending you a sign using your lucky number. You may see your lucky number in some places and that would mean a good thing because your spirit guide put it there for you to see and know that it is there for a reason. You may even hear your favorite song on the radio while having a bad day and it is a way for our spirit guide to cheer us up. They may also be direct and show you a dream on how to handle a current situation you are having. Our spirit guide is actively guiding us every day even without us noticing and it is our job to be more aware of it.

Meditate Everyday

Meditation started thousands of years ago and it is created to help us deepen our understanding of the sacred and mystical forces of life. Meditation is a mind and body activity that produces a tranquil mind that allows us to be more focused and it increases not only our self-awareness but also our awareness of our surroundings. While being in the state of deep relaxation caused by meditation, it helps us manage our stress in life and reduces the negative emotions in our body which in turn removes negative energies around us. Meditation also heightens our senses and improves our psychic abilities. During meditation is also the best time to communicate with your spirit guide.

Before you start meditating, you should first find a comfortable and quiet place for you to meditate in. Then find a comfortable sitting or standing position for you. Meditation is about finding the balance between relaxation and focus, being too relaxed can make you lose focus and being too focused would not allow you to be relaxed so you need to find the spot that is just right for you because not everyone is the same as everybody else. After finding the perfect position for you, it is recommended to close your eyes to help with your focus and then go for long deep breaths. Visualizing an object or a tranquil place can help with your focus and improves your clairvoyant sight. You can also ask your spirit guide to send a visual image in your mind to help with your meditation. Doing this every day will surely improve your life and help you develop your psychic abilities.

Being In Nature

Our environment directly affects our mind and body, it can increase or reduce our stress level depending on the environment that we are in. It is because of the negative and positive energies in our environment. We absorb our environment's energy and in turn, we release the same energy that we absorb. That is why we should be mindful of our environment and spend more time in a positive environment such as nature.

Being in nature or even simply viewing scenes of nature using our mind can help reduce anger and other negative feelings and increase pleasant feelings and help produce positive energy. Being exposed to nature not only improves our mind but also our body. Of course, being in nature is always better than just viewing scenes of it in our mind but it can also help, just do not forget to allocate a portion of your time to actually being in nature. Psychic empaths can be overwhelmed by the emotions and sensations that they feel and nature helps them soothe their mind by providing a calming space to rest and recover. Hiking in the forest or walking by the shore are some examples but you can also simply stay in a garden or rest under a tree.

Rest

When we think of resting the first thing that comes to mind is physical resting or resting our body by sleeping or taking a nap. Physical rest can also mean taking a short break from your work and taking a couple of long deep breaths outside. Having more energy physically is the result of physical resting. But aside from physical rest, we also have other types of resting such as mental rest, social rest, creative rest, and emotional rest.

1. **Mental Rest**

   Mental rest is about doing something to rest your mind, our mind is usually working nonstop and it badly needs a rest. An example of mental rest is meditating, meditation helps clear our mind of things to think about and it will be rested that way.

2. **Social Rest**

   Socializing can be very exhausting especially to psychic empaths because they are sensitive to being around other people. So, taking a break from meeting other people and spending alone time with yourself is needed to restore your energy.

3. Creative Rest

You may not notice it but you probably are always using your creativity on something like brainstorming on what design your room is going to have when you renovate it or planning for a theme of a birthday party for one of your friends and family. That can be very tiring and you will be in need of a creative rest. Give yourself a small break from all the creative thinking and go to a place that brings you inspiration like going for a walk in a calm forest or reading a good book to replenish your drained creative resources and take the pressure of creating out of your mind.

4. Emotional Rest

Being sad is very emotionally draining, ever wonder why you are tired after a sad situation has happened like when you got fired from work or you received a piece of very bad news like news of a loved one being in danger or them dying. That could leave you with no motivation to work or even do something as simple as leaving your room. It is because we are emotionally tired and need emotional rest. You are able to get emotional rest by unloading all your emotional feelings by talking to a willing listener and then continue talking to avoid more emotional tiredness in the future. That could mean talking to a close friend who will listen to you and not judge you and whom you can be yourself 100% or scheduling a visit for a regular therapy session from a therapist that you trust.

Rest is very important especially to psychics because we exert more energy than a normal person, so make sure to take plenty of rest because you cannot develop your psychic abilities if you do not have the energy to do it.

Psychic Protection

Energies from our day-to-day life can be overwhelming to us psychics because we are more sensitive to negative energies and negative atmospheres. Meeting people that emit negative energy or being in a place that is filled with negative energy could leave us feeling mentally and physically drained because we can feel and absorb the negative energies that are coming from them. Psychic protection is important for us to keep the positive energies that we have and for it to not be tainted with the negative energies around us. Keeping us away from negative energies and preserving our positive energies is the main point of psychic protection, it can be done by staying away from negative energy sources like people with negative personalities or places that are filled with negative energies such as a cluttered workplace or a home that is unorganized and unclean.

How To Remove Negative Influences

Removing negative influences is important for the well-being of a psychic empath because it can affect them more than a normal person due to their ability to sense the negative energies. Psychic empaths are more sensitive to negative energy that is coming from negative influences and to protect them from it, first, we need to identify these negative influences. It could be a negative person, a negative environment, or even a negative mindset from the psychic itself.

Spend Less Time With Negative Individuals

The first negative thing to protect a psychic from are negative individuals. They may be hard to avoid because we cannot control other people and negative individuals are drawn to the positive energy that is emanating from a psychic. Negative individuals usually have problems that they do not want to face so they release their negativity in some other shape or form, that is why they release so much negative energy. And sadly, for psychics, those types of people are drawn to us because of all the positive energy that is coming from us.

Negative individuals are like a tomato with a rotten part that is placed in a basket together with other fresh tomatoes. The rotten part of the tomato will spread out and infect the other good tomatoes. To avoid getting infected, the best way to deal with it is to separate the rotten tomato so that the other fresh tomatoes are not going to be contaminated. That is also the same with people, if we spend less time with negative individuals, we are less likely to be affected by their negative energies. It would be ideal to completely avoid them but you cannot avoid them you can just spend less time with them.

To start, you should identify which individuals are producing negative energies. They are usually the ones who are always angry for no good reason, the ones that invade your space without your consent and take up a lot of your time for doing things that are not important to you or things that you do not enjoy, and generally, they are the ones that make you feel uncomfortable or makes you less productive because you will feel drained around them. You should protect yourself from them by setting a boundary. Spend less time with them and spend more time on yourself to recover all the positive energy that you have lost while being with them. Also do not feel guilty about what you are doing, it is for your well-being and the well-being of those individuals around you because if you spend less time around them maybe they can face their problems on their own instead of escaping from them.

Stay Away From Negative Environments

People are not the only ones that produce negative energy, negative environments are also needed to be avoided by a psychic because they also produce negative energy. These negative environments can include places that are too loud and noisy because they may irritate you and make you lose focus. Places that are dirty, cluttered, and unorganized can also negatively affect a psychic, these could be places that you hang out in, your workplace, or even your own home.

Staying away from these negative environments can help you regain your positive energies or you can clean and organize the place if you are able to, especially if it is your workplace or your home because it would be hard to stay away from it. Adding plants to those places can also improve it because nature is a soothing and restorative place not just for normal people but also for us psychics.

Stop Negative Talk/Thought About Yourself

All of us have experienced having negative thoughts about ourselves and negative self-talking. It is when we tell ourselves or think to ourselves that we are not good enough and we should not attempt something to avoid failure or for us to be safe. Sometimes that voice is downright mean and says something like "you will never do anything right" or "you will never be good at anything you are doing".

Those negative self-talk and negative self-thoughts can negatively impact a normal person and can negatively impact a psychic even more because negative self-thinking and negative self-talk both produce negative energy and drain the positive energy from a psychic. It can hinder your progress and your ability to do something because the more that you tell yourself that you cannot do something, the more that you will believe it and you will not accomplish anything.

You will be afraid to try because you believe that you cannot do it even if, in fact, you can actually do it.

You can stop negative self-talk and negative self-thoughts by doing the following:

1. **Notice Negative Self-talks and Negative Self-thoughts**

    First, noticing when you are starting to have negative self-thoughts or you are negative self-talking. A good rule of thumb to determine if you are negative self-talking or having negative self-thoughts is if you are saying something to yourself that you would not normally say to your friends or family.

2. **Acknowledge Your Negative Self-talks and Negative Self-thoughts**

    When you feel like you are starting to have negative self-thoughts you should acknowledge it and not run from it. Do not ignore it when you are having negative self-thoughts. You have to admit that you are having them before you can face up to your problem. It is not easy to accept that you are having doubts or that you are afraid but you will never put a stop to your negative self-talk and negative self-thoughts if you do not acknowledge them.

3. Find The Cause Of Your Negative Self-talks and Negative Self-thoughts

Take some time to consider what is causing your negative self-thoughts and negative self-talk so that you can address them and try to do something to stop them. Is it because you are having self-doubt? Is it because you are afraid? Did something happen that made you lose your self-confidence? If you are doubting yourself, tell yourself that it is going to be fine, that everyone can fail, and the only way to know if you can do it or not is to try doing what you need to do. If you do fail, it is okay, you can always try again and you can always try to be better.

4. Avoid Perfectionism

Stop expecting everything to be perfect especially when you are just starting out. Always remember to tell yourself that no one is perfect and it is okay to fail. Your flaws and imperfections are a part of who you are and everyone has them. If you make a mistake, it is okay to try again and try to do better. It is better to fail and try again because you will eventually succeed instead of just worrying and not getting anything done because you are too afraid to try. Once you accept your imperfections and you move forward with them you will become more self-confident and more successful not just in your life but also in your psychic journey.

Turn Negative Talk To Positive

Stopping your negative self-talk is just one way to deal with it. Another approach is to turn your negative talks into positive talks. It is harder to do but it will give you better results at improving your positive energy. Here are some helpful steps to turn your negative self-talk into positive:

1. **Write Down Your Negative Self-talks**

   The first step you need to do to turn negative talk into positive is to write down all your negative talks in a day as soon as they start occurring. For a whole day, pay attention to all your thoughts and try to recognize which of them are negative self-talk and write it down in a notebook or type it into your phone's notes.

2. **Review What You Wrote At The End Of The Day**

   At the end of the day when you are not in the heat of the moment that brought those negative self-talk, try to review everything that you wrote. See which of those thoughts are really true and which of them is just you being too hard on yourself. Would you say what you wrote to a friend? If not, then why do you think is it okay to say it to yourself? It is not okay, right? It is just making you feel bad about yourself.

3. Replace The Negative Thoughts With Positive Ones

After reviewing the things that you wrote at the end of the day, you should try to think of something to counter the negative thoughts that you are having. For example, instead of saying that you missed a gym session today and you are a failure for doing so, say something like "Even though I missed a gym session today, I have been consistent with it before that, and I will make sure to not miss my next session and be more consistent with it." That will counter the negative thought that you had because of missing a gym session and it will give you the inspiration to do better next time. No one is perfect in this world and you should not pressure yourself to be perfect. It is okay to make mistakes and learn from them. What is not okay is to make a mistake then beat yourself for it and stop trying. So be sure to fight those negative thoughts and replace them with positive ones.

Be Yourself

Pretending to be somebody who you are not is a bad thing and could make you produce negative energies which are bad for a psychic. Here are some steps to help you be who you are and live a happy life so you can produce more positive energy and protect yourself from the negative energies of the world.

1. **Discover Yourself And Find Out Who You Really Are**

   The first thing you need to do is to find out who you are and define yourself on your own terms. You cannot be yourself if you do not know who you are and you do not understand yourself.

2. **Appreciate Yourself And Be Confident On Who You Are**

   No matter what you discover about yourself, even if it is weird, you should not be shy of yourself. Be confident in who you really are and appreciate yourself. Do not compare yourself with anybody because everybody is different and you are special in your own way.

3. **Forgive Your Mistakes And Stop Being Negative About Yourself**

   Forgive yourself if you ever make a mistake, nobody is perfect. You cannot help it, every one of us is going to make a mistake sooner or later because we are just humans. So, you should stop being negative about yourself and forgive the mistakes that you made. Negative self-talk is not going to accomplish anything and will just make things worse, that is why you should avoid it.

4. Learn From Your Mistakes

After forgiving yourself for your mistakes, you should think about the wrong thing that you did and try to find something that you can learn from it. What can you change about your actions that will change the outcome if ever you are in the same situation again? Look for that information and try to better yourself.

5. Do Not Worry About How Others View You

My final tip is to not worry about how others view you and just be who you are. If you worry about what they think of you, you will subconsciously be someone that you think would please the other person. It would mean that we are back at the start and you are not being yourself again. You should always put what you want on top of your priority list and not what others want.

Have A Positive Lifestyle

Having a positive lifestyle would keep negative energies away from a psychic and will help keep your positive energy safe from the negativity of the world around us. Here are some tips to help you live a positive life and protect yourself from the negative energies of others.

1. **Smile More Often**

   A smile is a powerful tool we can use to spread positivity not just for others but also for ourselves. Even a fake smile can have a positive effect on your mind and body. Try looking in a mirror and smile at yourself even if it is a fake smile. You will feel a bit lighter and more positive even with a fake smile and later on that fake smile will turn into a true smile eventually. Smiling at others will help spread the positivity around you and it will make them smile too which will then make the others around them smile. A smile is contagious and very helpful in living a positive lifestyle.

2. **Focus On The Positive Things**

   Instead of crying over spilled beans, we should focus on what is left and make the most out of it. Focusing on the positive things will make us much happier and will mitigate the effects of negativity in our life. Instead of thinking that the glass is half empty, we should think of it as half full glass which not only has something in it but also has enough room to fill it up even more.

3. **Write Down Things That You Are Grateful About**

   Writing down things that you are grateful for will help remind you that you have plenty of positive things that are going on with your life. Read it every day and continue to add more stuff to it that you think is something you should be grateful for. It will help you focus more on the positive things in your life instead of moping around over the negative things in your life.

4. Spend More Time With Positive People

Negativity is contagious because being around negative people will also bring you negative energy but that is also the case for positive people. Being around positive people brings positive energy so you should spend more time with positive people. These people are the ones who are happy and fun to be around. They lighten the atmosphere with their positive aura and bring smiles to everyone around them. Spending more time with them will help you turn into a positive person yourself.

5. Always Start Your Day On A Positive Note

Starting your day on a positive note like saying something like "This day is going to be great" even though we do not actually know how your day is going to be. It will still help you have a more positive outlook on your day. You will notice more positive things happening around you and in turn making your day actually great. You can also listen to a happy song or playlist to start your day happy. Sharing a compliment and a smile will help spread positivity at the start of your day and it will be harder for the negativity to affect you.

6. Stop Worrying About The Future

Our future is never certain and worrying about the future is just going to bring us stress and negative energies. You should focus on the present and just worry about things as they happen. Being ready for anything that the future holds and keeping an open mind is the best way to handle your future. Be prepared for anything that the world will throw at you and keep being positive and everything will be alright.

7. Exercise Regularly, Eat Nutritious Foods, And Have A Good Sleeping Schedule

Taking care of your body is as important as taking care of your mind. Exercising regularly is a great way to keep your body strong and healthy. Eating nutritious foods will give you the energy to be active and happy. Having a good sleeping schedule is also important so you feel well-rested and not feel sluggish. Keep your body healthy and your mood will automatically improve and it will help you live a positive life easier.

Clairvoyant Healing

Clairvoyant healing is the ability to heal the energies around you which involves the transfer of energy from the healer to the person they are trying to heal. Clairvoyant healing can heal physical injuries by enhancing the receiver's energy which promotes self-healing and strengthening the body's immune system. It can also heal a relationship between two people by getting rid of the negative energies that are affecting the relationship and the two people that are involved.

There are many techniques that can be used when you are performing clairvoyant healing. A simple touch, acupuncture, prayers, chants, herbs, oils, and crystals are just a few methods that are proven effective sometimes by other psychics. Most of the time, these methods are accompanied by visualization. It is natural for us to visualize something that is connected to our intentions and desires. For example, when you are hungry you may start to visualize the food that you want to eat. When you intend to heal yourself or someone else, it is normal for you to visualize the person getting better, the sickness leaving the person you are healing, or their problems leaving them or getting fixed.

Healing Physical Sickness

When someone gets a bruise or cut on their body, after some time that injury will heal itself even if it is not treated. It is because all of us have our own life force healing energy inside us. A psychic can amplify the effects of the healing energy inside us and help a person heal a physical injury or sickness. A psychic can also share the healing energy inside him to heal the person that needs help. The healer just needs to focus and visualize the energies that he wants to manipulate, he can speed up the healing properties of the person that is being healed, or he can run his healing energies to the other person to heal him. The psychic can also visualize the sickness leaving the body of the other person for more effective treatment. Crystals can also help while the psychic is meditating, he just needs to hold the crystals and let the other person hold them afterward.

Healing Relationships

A relationship is just like a person, it can be affected by all kinds of energy that can have an effect on the health of the relationship. The two people that are involved in a relationship can bring all kinds of emotions and energies that can make the relationship stronger or tear it apart. Healing a relationship does not always mean that the relationship is going to be saved and all problems are going to go away. Performing a relationship healing can end up with the termination of the relationship if that is what is best for both the parties involved with it. What is guaranteed is that both persons that are in the relationship will be more honest with each other and they will both be peaceful and all the negativity that is affecting the relationship will disappear. To perform relationship healing, you need to visualize the two persons in a relationship and assign a clear object to them. You can assign a clear flower for example. Then try to see a color on that clear flower and try to find the similarities and differences between the two flowers. The next thing to do is to command all foreign energies to be released from the two flowers. After all the foreign energies have exited, you should choose an energy that you would like to bring into the two flowers that could positively affect their relationship such as peace, happiness, love, and passion. Once the process is complete, you should clear your mind and start meditating to calm yourself and relax.

Telepathy

Telepathy is one of the most powerful psychic abilities in which it enables the psychic to send and receive thoughts or feelings from another person using only the power of the mind without using any physical interactions. Users of this psychic ability are often called mind readers or telepaths. Telepathy can be categorized into these two kinds: Telepathic Communication which is the ability to send thoughts and feelings using the psychic's mind into another psychic's mind, and Telepathic Perception which is the ability to receive thoughts and feelings using the psychic's mind from another psychic's mind. There are three major types of telepathy: Instinctual Telepathy, Dream Telepathy, and Mental Telepathy.

Instinctual Telepathy

Instinctual Telepathy is the type of telepathy that most of us have, it is when a psychic senses the feelings or needs of someone that is nearby via a mental connection. It uses the area around our solar plexus which is the center of our instincts and emotions. This is where the term "gut feel" came from. This type of telepathy is something that we often experience with people that we have a strong emotional and mental bond with like our loved ones such as our parents, spouse, siblings, or very close friends. The most noticeable example of instinctual telepathy involves sensing intense emotions when someone is in an emergency, serious distress, or death.

Dream Telepathy

Dream telepathy is the type of telepathy that occurs when a psychic communicates with someone's mind or receives a telepathic transmission while being in a dream. An example of this is when you have a dream about someone close to you being sad and attempting to overdose himself with sleeping pills while in fact it is happening in real life or it is about to happen. This is a sign of telepathic transmission that you have received by having insights into that someone's mind. Another example is when you meet a friend in your dream and you tell them something then when you wake up and meet that person in real life, you both had the same dream and he received your message. You might think that it is a coincidence but that is a sign that you sent a telepathic transmission to your friend.

Mental Telepathy

Mental telepathy is the type of telepathy that is the hardest type of telepathy to perform because it requires a lot of practice and dedication. Mental telepathy is the direct transmission of information from the psychic's mind to another mind. While most humans and animals have instinctual telepathy, mental telepathy requires the opening of our "third eye" which opens up the mind to the world beyond our five senses. The third eye is the center of telepathy and other psychic abilities. The main difference between instinctual telepathy and mental telepathy is that instinctual telepathy occurs naturally and sometimes without even us noticing while the mental telepathy is deliberate and intentional.

How To Practice and Develop Your Telepathic Abilities

If you want to develop your telepathic abilities, it would require consistent practice and the following steps:

1. **Believe in Yourself and Believe in Telepathy**

   The first thing you need to do before being able to communicate telepathically is to believe in yourself that you can do it and to believe that telepathy exists. Remove all the doubts in your heart and mind and surrender yourself to the powers of your third eye.

2. **Find A Willing Partner That You Have Strong Bonds With**

   Find someone that you have strong bonds with and have an open mind who also believes in telepathy. If one of you has doubts, you may have a hard time achieving mental communication. Your partner can be a close friend, your spouse, or one of your family members.

3. Focus Your Thoughts

The first step to take is to calm your body and mind then focus your thoughts. Find a comfortable position and start to meditate. Tell your partner to also do the same to receive your telepathic transmission.

4. Imagine The Person You Are Communicating With

The next thing to do while you are focused is to imagine the person you are trying to communicate with telepathically. Close your eyes and try to picture your partner and every detail about him as close as you possibly can like the way he looks, how tall he is, and every specific detail that you can visualize.

5. Visualize The Message You Are Trying To Send

After Imagining that the person you are trying to communicate telepathically with is in front of you, you should visualize the message you are trying to send. You can start with a simple object like a pen, try to visualize it as detailed as possible and focus your mind only on it. Imagine the object's shape, its size, its color, its weight, its length, and all the other characteristics that you can imagine and transmit that mental image to your telepathic partner.

6. Tell The Receiver To Write Down What Came To Their Mind

After you have sent the telepathic message you are trying to send, your partner should remain calm and focused until they feel that the thought has entered their mind. Then you should ask them to write down what is the thought that came to their mind in complete detail. You should also write the message you are trying to send your partner.

7. Compare The Results

After you both write the thought, try to compare your results and see if you both have the same things you have written down. At first, you may not be successful but do not get discouraged because with practice you will soon be able to communicate telepathically. Just try again and practice until you can consistently tell what each other is thinking about.

How Can You Tell The Difference Between Telepathy And Imagination

Finding the difference between telepathy and imagination is as simple as creating an experiment with your telepathy partner. You can also confirm if your vision is telepathy or imagination by asking the people involved in your vision. For example, when you suddenly saw a picture in your mind that shows your spouse in a dangerous situation. You should definitely call her immediately and ask her to confirm but do not suddenly ask her questions that will freak her out like "Did you have an accident, are you okay?". Instead, you can ask her for other specific details that can be connected with your vision like "Where are you right now?" or "What are you currently doing?". After that, you can compare her answers if it is connected to the vision you saw.

Do not worry because you will only be confused about it in the beginning. Once you get comfortable with your ability you will be able to tell right away if it is just your imagination or it is a telepathic transmission.

Opening Your Third Eye

Opening our third eye is an essential step to unlocking our sleeping psychic abilities. Having an opened third eye is required to perceive the world around us in a spiritual manner. If your third eye is not yet opened, you should try and open it as soon as you can because it will be a major step in your psychic ability development journey. Your third eye will help you with developing all your other psychic abilities.

What Is A Third Eye

Our third eye is located in our forehead right above the middle of our eyebrows. The third eye is the key to most of the psychic abilities that we possess, it is the center of our energies and chakras related to clarity, imagination, intuition, concentration, spiritual perception, and universal connection. While our two physical eyes see the physical world, our third eye sees the world beyond that, it sees the spiritual world which is the world that contains the secrets of our universe, the things that physical science cannot explain.

Steps to Opening Your Third Eye

Opening your third eye is not an easy feat. It requires dedication and complete focus on your goal. Believing in the higher powers that govern our universe is essential and also believing in yourself. With these steps, I will help you open your third eye and awaken you to a world of infinite possibilities.

1. **Focus Your Concentration On The Area Of Your Third Eye**

    The first thing to do is to focus and concentrate all your energies in the area of your third eye. It is located in our forehead above the middle of our eyebrows. Find a comfortable position and close your eyes, then feel your energies and concentrate them in your third eye to open it. This may not work right away but with your continuous efforts and determination, you will be rewarded with an opened third eye.

2. **Breathe Slowly And Calmly**

    After finding the perfect position for you, breathe slowly and calmly to relax yourself and help you focus more on opening your third eye. You should find the perfect balance of relaxation and focus to achieve your goal of opening your third eye.

3. **Pay Attention To Your Visions And Dreams**

Our dreams can sometimes be disoriented and confusing but always pay attention to your dreams because it may give you clues on opening your third eye. It is recommended to write down your dreams and make a dream journal to track your dreams and try to find a pattern that can help you. Visions are also one to look out for, sometimes we are given a vision and we thought it is just our imagination but it can be our spirit guide helping you achieve your goal. So do not just dismiss it as your imagination because it could be something helpful.

4. **Take Care Of Your Body And Eat Nutritious Foods**

Of course, we should also take care of our body because it is our spirit's vessel. A body that is well taken care of is going to be a better temple for your spirit and can help improve your energies and chakras. Food choices are very important for chakra alignment because our food choices govern our energy. If you are always eating junk food it will be a lot harder for you to concentrate and open your third eye, so eat healthy foods instead.

5. **Meditate With Crystals Or Essential Oils**

Crystals are a great spiritual tool that can help us open our third eye. You can try placing a crystal on the area of your third eye, which is in your forehead, while you are laying down comfortably and focus your breathing and your energy on the crystal to help you focus on opening your third eye. You can also hold the crystal in your hands while you are meditating. Using essential oils together with your crystal can help you even further. Diffusing essential oils that have scents like lavender, pine, frankincense, or sandalwood help gently stimulate your pineal glands which help in opening your third eye.

How To Know When Your Third Eye Is Opened

There is no specific time on how long you need in order to open your third eye. It varies from person to person depending on their psychic energies. Some believe that it can take years to a lifetime of practice to open our third eye and some believe you can open it in a short amount of time like a week or a month. The most important thing is to not rush it or try to force anything. Focus on your practice and do whatever feels right for you instead of worrying about a deadline.

To know when your third eye is open, the answer is simple. You will become more aware of the field of energy around you and you will gain access to a higher consciousness which will allow you to receive guidance messages and visions from your spirit guide. This will also help you gain psychic abilities such as telepathy and you will have heightened intuitions.

Connecting With Spirit Guides

Being able to connect with your spirit guide is a great psychic ability to have. Not only are they going to guide and support you, but your spirit guide will also help you help other people that are lost in life and in need of helping. We need this loving and guiding presence that is filled with love now more than ever because of all the chaos and negativity that is happening in the world. Do not be afraid to call upon your spirit guide anytime you need them because they are always with us. Just be careful to not accidentally call an evil spirit, make sure to communicate with them and confirm their intentions before you welcome them.

What Is A Spirit Guide

A spirit guide is a spiritual entity that acts as a psychic's protector and gives guidance. Some of the spirit guides have been with you even before you were born and some of them came to you as you needed them at different moments in your life or they can come when you request their guidance. A spirit guide holds energy and has the ability to communicate with us using the energy around us to send us messages or visions. They are also filled with the energy of love and peace that helps us feel at ease whenever they are supporting us and giving us guidance.

Types Of Spirit Guides

Spirit guides come in different forms and types, and they can be one of the following:

1. **Deceased Loved Ones Or Ancestors**

    Our deceased loved ones can be our spirit guide if they decide to stay here on earth and be your spirit guide and actively assist you in your life endeavors. This could be a loved one you know or it could also be one of your ancestors that you do not even know but wants to help you in your life because you have similarities.

2. **Spirit Animals**

    A Spirit Animal could be a pet you had before but has already passed away or it could be any animal that has something to teach you. They can show up in your dreams or they can appear in front of you while you are meditating. They can also send you a sign by appearing in a picture that you see somewhere in your everyday life such as, an advertisement on a car ride or in a mug of your coworker.

3. **Ascended Masters**

    Ascended Masters were once human but they attained eternal awakening and they ascended to the spirit realm. An example of a well-known ascended master is Buddha, who went on a journey to find spiritual enlightenment. They guide other humans into a better path so we can also attain spiritual enlightenment.

4. **Other Helpful Spirits**

    These are people who have passed away in the past but they decided to stay behind and guide other people that they may be interested in. Some just wanted to help and others wanted to find a friend. Just make sure that the spirit you connect to is not a bad spirit.

5. **Guardian Angels**

    Each of us has a guardian angel that is assigned to us exclusively that is usually there to observe and protect us from the negativity of the world. They are with us before we are even born; they are watching over us and protecting us at all times.

6. **Other Helper Angels**

    This type of angel is the one that is not assigned to a specific person so they go around and find someone to help and guide. They may choose to stay with you for a while or only after they are finished with a specific lesson they wanted to teach you.

7. **Archangels**

    Archangels are the strongest type of angels and they have the most powerful energy among all the angels.

They are the leaders of the Angel world and each of them has a specialty. Archangel Raphael, for example, specializes in healing and can work with multiple persons at once.

How To Connect With A Spirit Guide

Connecting with a spirit guide has plenty of benefits and all psychics should be connecting with their spirit guide to ask for guidance. Here are some helpful tips to help you connect with your spirit guide.

1. **Trust In Your Psychic Abilities And Concentrate**

   You should believe in yourself and in your ability to call upon your spirit guide. Know that every one of us has a spirit guide filled with the energy of positivity and love that is always present to help and guide us. The more that you trust in your psychic ability, the more that it will manifest and you will be able to connect with your spirit guide easily.

2. **Ask For Your Spirit Guide**

   We often forget that we have a spirit guide that is always with us. Because of our busy everyday life, it is really easy to slip one's mind that we have this guidance. You should get in the habit of asking for your spirit guide's help and guidance. The more that you ask for your spirit guide's support, the more that you will receive its guidance. Think about all the things you need help with and do not be afraid to ask your spirit guide for help because they will be more than happy to help us because it is what they want to do.

3. Listen To Your Spirit Guide

The way a psychic can listen to his spirit guide is by meditation. When you meditate, you enter a state of complete focus and relaxation. Everything around you will be quiet and your mind will become clear. This will be the perfect time for you to listen to your spirit guide for their wisdom and guidance. We have to slow down our vibrations so that we can be aligned with the presence of our spirit guide. When we line up our energies to the frequency of peace and love, we can easily connect with the message that our spirit guide is sending to us.

4. Ask For A Sign From Your Spirit Guide

Our spirit guide shows us signs often and sometimes we are not even aware of it. You can ask your spirit guide for a sign to guide you towards anything you want. If you need guidance about a decision that you are not sure about, or you just want confirmation that what you are doing is correct, you can ask your spirit guide to show you a sign. Just let whatever comes to your mind first to be the sign, allow it to come to you naturally and do not force it. You may receive a sign in the form of a song that you hear, an animal, or a thing that symbolizes something that is related to the thing that you ask guidance about.

5. Pay Attention To The Signs That You Are Receiving

Of course, after asking for a sign from your spirit guide, you should pay attention to your surroundings and try to notice the sign that you are asking for. Paying attention and looking out for the sign that you asked for is not about being demanding, you should not go around all day asking your spirit guidance where your sign is. Instead, you should be patient and simply allow yourself to be open to the wonders of your spirit guide's guidance and wait for the sign that you asked for.

6. Always Be Grateful To Your Spirit Guide

You should be grateful to your spirit guide for all the support and guidance that they are giving you. Instead of always being in a state of neediness, it is a good idea to sometimes say thank you to our spirit guides. We should appreciate our spirit guide because even without our knowledge, they are out there supporting us and sending us guidance to help us with our life. Your gratitude towards them will make your relationship with your spirit guide stronger and it will help keep your spirit guide present with you all the time because they know that you are welcoming them.

Communicate With Your Spirit Guide As Much As You Can

Once you are comfortable with connecting with your spirit guide, you should communicate with it as often as you can because the more you communicate with your spirit guide, the more you will rely on it. The more that you ask for divine guidance and you surrender yourself to it, the more miracles will happen to your life. Your spirit guide always wants to connect with you because it makes them happy that they are able to help people. Communicating with your spirit guide does not always have to be you asking for a favor, you can speak to them and thank them for all the help and guidance they did for you to better your life.

CHAPTER 2: UNDERSTANDING PSYCHIC EMPATHS

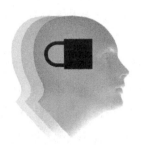 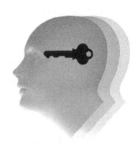

What Is A Psychic Empath?

A Psychic Empath is a person that has the capacity to see and feel the emotions of other people and what they are feeling, even more than their own. They can see other people's energy vibrations, sense their aura, and even feel their physical pain. However, do not confuse the psychic form of empathy with the basic human emotion of empathy. Most normal people can feel empathy and they can understand and feel what other people are experiencing. What is different is that a psychic empath has the ability to pick up another person's feelings of fear, pain, or joy without the need for visual or verbal indications.

A psychic empath can be overwhelmed by the countless number of emotions that are being bombarded to them by all the people around them, that is why it is important to understand them and learn how to adjust to your ability if you are one of them. Different types of empaths specialize in different things, here are the seven different types of psychic empaths:

Physical Empath

A physical empath is a type of psychic empath that is more inclined with the physical actions and physical feelings of other people. If the people around them are injured, have an illness, have a headache, or experiencing some other health conditions, a physical empath can experience similar discomfort. Displaying the symptoms of other people's illnesses is a common problem for physical empaths, so it is ideal to spend more time with people who are healthy and happy to offset the negativity that the other people are giving you. It is also important to manage the downside of your psychic ability by setting a healthy boundary and learn to say no to spending time with people who are bringing negative energies to your life.

Emotional Empath

An Emotional empath can pick up on the emotional energies of other people and they are likely to mirror these feelings. This means that they can feel genuine joy and happiness for the success of a loved one. On the other hand, if an emotional empath is around emotional vampires or people who are filled with negative emotions and have negative personalities, they are going to suffer and feel drained.

People who are constant talkers and are not interested in other people's feelings, people who are control freaks and try to dictate how other people are supposed to act and feel, people who are narcissists and make everything about them and disregard other people, people who are always playing to be the victim even if they are actually not and they are just over exaggerating, and people who are drama queens and make a deal out of every small incident in their life are the types of people an emotional empath should try to avoid to preserve the empath's well-being.

Intuitive Empath

An Intuitive empath is similar to an emotional empath in a sense because they can also pick up emotional energies from other people, but what sets aside an intuitive empath is that they can also see what is beyond the surface-level feelings. An intuitive empath can often tell when someone is telling lies or whether they are telling the truth. A high-level intuitive empath can sometimes feel what is going to happen before they even occur and can answer questions about someone's self that even that person does not know the answer to. They can understand people who do not even understand themselves.

Dream Empath

A dream can sometimes feel like an impossible riddle to solve. They can be confusing and even feel disoriented on some occasions, but a dream empath is gifted in being able to understand and unravel the mysteries that are hidden in our dreams. A dream empath can avoid the obstacles of physical reality and gather intuitive wisdom from the universe while they are asleep.

A dream empath specializes in being able to decipher the meaning of their own dream. Unlike an average person who forgets a dream instantly as soon as they wake up, a dream empath has the ability to remember every single detail of their dream. As they recall their dreams, they will often gain wisdom and guidance from it. In addition to being able to understand and learn from their own dreams, a dream empath can also help understand the meaning of another person's dream.

Animal Empath

This type of psychic empaths are the ones who are close to animals. They can often be seen sharing stories with an animal or simply playing with animals more often than they spend time with other people. Animal empaths may have multiple animals living in their home and they treat them like family members instead of just pets.

An animal empath can intuitively sense an animal's needs and emotions. An animal empath can often be able to communicate with animals, both understanding the animal and being able to make the animal understand them also using the power of their mind. Most animal empaths decide to live a vegan lifestyle because they cannot tolerate any cruelty towards animals. They argue that animals are also sentient beings that are capable of feeling emotions and have the right to live just like us human beings.

Plant Empath

A plant empath has a natural green thumb and they are in tune with flowers, plants, and trees. Plant empaths can form a connection similar to the connections that an emotional or physical empath can experience with other people. They have the ability to sense and find out what a plant needs to grow and be healthy, and they can even communicate with them and hear their thoughts. Being surrounded by plants can also be beneficial for a plant empath because they bring peace and tranquility. Plant empaths are known for being skilled at spiritual healing and for being very compassionate people.

Earth Empath

Earth empaths are similar to plant empaths because they are also in tune with nature. However, earth empaths are connected to our world as a whole, this includes mountains, forests, and the ocean. A natural disaster such as earthquakes and forest fires can make an earth empath feel pain. They can also sense a severe storm before it happens. An earth empath loves the outdoors and can flourish when they are exposed to natural energy sources such as the crashing waves on a beach, a raging waterfall, and beautiful unobstructed sunrise and sunset. However, environmental toxins and pollutants can harm an earth empath more than they affect an ordinary person who is not spiritually connected to the earth.

How A Psychic Empath Feels

A psychic empath is a highly sensitive person who can experience other people's emotions using the power of their spiritual energy. Psychic empaths have the special ability to absorb and feel the emotions of other people which, in most cases, makes them extremely compassionate, understanding, and caring people. Here are some examples of how a psychic empath feels:

<u>Highly Sensitive</u>

Due to the ability of a psychic empath to be aware of other people's feelings and emotions, they can become highly sensitive to it and it can affect their own feelings and emotions. Psychic empaths tend to mirror another person's current emotions even if they are not doing it on purpose. The energy that a person releases, be it positive or negative, can be absorbed by a psychic empath and in turn, make them feel the same way the other person is feeling. A sad person that releases negative energy can make a psychic empath also feel sad and down, while a happy and positive person who releases positive energy can make a psychic empath feel happy and energized. Staying away and spending less time with a person that releases negative energies is beneficial for a psychic empath's well-being. Meanwhile, spending more time with happy people that releases positive energy will also bring positive effects to the psychic empath's life.

Hate Conflict

Psychic empaths really hate conflicts because it can be very draining for them due to the fact that they are highly sensitive to emotions and energies. Conflicts will cause psychic empaths to deplete their positive energy to help solve it. Even if they are just being around the conflict and not involved with it, psychic empaths can still absorb the negative energy that is coming from the person having the said conflict and make the empath feel tired. It is advisable for a psychic empath to avoid getting into conflicts or staying away from the person who has conflicts. If you cannot avoid the person that has a conflict, you can try to help them solve it or find someone who can help them solve the conflict. Not only will this help you stay away from the negative energies that are coming from the conflict, but it can also help you feel fulfilled after the person solves his problem. They will come to you happy and thank you for the help you did for them and that will help you recover the positive energies that you have used in dealing with the conflict.

Take Long To Process Emotions

Psychic empaths can take a long time to process emotions because they have more information to process, unlike an average person. Psychic empaths need to process their own emotions and the emotions of the people around them.

Sometimes, it may get confusing because they may confuse the emotion of other people as their own emotions because they can sense the emotion unintentionally. They may suddenly feel sad and think that it is their emotion, but it can just be them sensing someone that is around them who is feeling sad. It is recommended to spend some time alone with yourself so that you can figure out if it is your own emotion or you are just mistaking the emotion of others as your own. Being alone also helps psychic empaths to rest and recharge their energies.

High Sensory Stimulation

High sensory stimulation is the input and sensation that a psychic empath receives when he activates and utilizes his sixth sense. It is like when you hear something with your ears or see something with your eyes, but this time it is the sensation that a psychic empath feels when they are receiving sensations related to the universe's spiritual energies. This may come from another person's emotions or even an animal's feelings. The earth also releases natural energies, it is the reason why we feel at ease when we are around nature.

High sensory stimulation can also be the feeling that you feel when you are meditating and communicating with your spirit guide. However, high sensory stimulation is not always positive. It is also the negative sensations that you feel when you are surrounded by negative energies coming from a negative environment or negative people. If you encounter negative stimulation, I suggest that you try to relax and focus on a different part of your surroundings. If you cannot do that, your only choice is to leave the area as soon as you can to minimize the effects of the negative energy on you. After leaving the area, you should calm yourself and take a rest. Meditation can also help if you have the chance and energy left to do it.

Loving And Compassionate

Having the ability to sense and understand other people's feelings and emotions naturally turns a psychic empath into a very compassionate and loving person. When you understand the reason for someone's behavior, it is easier for you to be compassionate towards them and you will be a much more loving person. Lots of people do not understand each other, that is why they tend to hate what the other person is doing because they do not know the reason as to why that person is behaving like that. It is understandable to feel angry and that the world is unfair when you spend so much attention and dedication and work so hard for something for a long time then you end up not getting what you wanted or even worse, someone you think who is not deserving gets it instead and with minimal effort. What we sometimes do not understand is maybe the other person also worked hard for it but the first person just did not see it. That misunderstanding can cause hate and produce negative energies and a psychic empath can prevent all that because they can sense and understand the emotions and feelings of the other person if they are the one in that situation.

Good At Connecting Dots

A psychic empath's intuition is highly sensitive, that is why they are good at figuring things out and connecting the dots. Psychic empaths can sense and understand the hidden information that is in the energies that surround them, this is the reason why they have a good intuition and can connect the dots more easily than a normal person without psychic abilities. A psychic empath's spirit guide can also give him a sign to help give him guidance in solving things for him or a person around him that needs help. Psychic empath's powers are not only used to help themselves but to also help the psychic empath help other people that need help and are willing to let the psychic empath help them.

Love Nature

Nature is a place that is calming and filled with tranquility. A psychic empath is drawn to nature because it releases plenty of positive natural energies that can help an empath relax and recover all the energies that they used up. Having a long walk on a shore at the beach, spending the night in the wilderness while camping, climbing on top of a high mountain are some of the activities you can do to help you be closer to nature and make you full of positive energies. Even a simple task like meditating on a small garden can also help. Having plants in your workplace or your home can also help improve the amount of positive energy that is surrounding the area.

Understanding Hypersensitivity

Being hypersensitive is one of the signs of being a psychic empath. They are deeply affected by strong scents, bright lights, loud noises, itchy clothing, and the amount of energy and emotions that they can feel around. They have intensified reactions to their surroundings and they can be overwhelmed by it more times than they would like. Because of this condition, it may be harder for them to multitask and they can become more stressed when there is a lot going on at once. People with hypersensitivity may be required to rest after being exposed to a lot of stimulation because it makes them tired and it drains their energy.

Hypersensitive people can also be very observant. If something changes around them, even if it is a very minor change, they will notice it. Are you in a bad mood but you are trying your best to hide it? A hypersensitive person will probably notice. Did you use a new laundry detergent, new shampoo for your hair, or new cologne? Someone with hypersensitivity will also notice it right away. They can notice even the slightest change around them and all of that noticing can make them very tired and lifeless at times.

Good communication is also key when dealing with people with hypersensitivity. They might try to ask you plenty of questions when they feel like there is something different about the way you are acting. Try to avoid making them guess and just tell them straight what exactly is wrong because they might end up drawing their own conclusions or they might be extremely stressed from not knowing if there is something wrong. It can be hard for you to express your feelings but try to do your best to make them understand especially if you are close to the person with hypersensitivity.

If you are one that has hypersensitivity, here are some helpful tips to help you on how to deal with your hypersensitivity.

Mind Your Own Business

Minding your own business is about letting go of the things you cannot control and focusing on the things that you can control. It is about taking responsibility for yourself and your own thoughts, actions, and words while letting others take responsibility for theirs. In many instances, we try to control other people and control the world around us, and basically, we try to control everything and everyone except for ourselves which is ironic because the only thing that we can surely control is ourselves. And even then, we do not have perfect control over ourselves. Since you are highly affected by a lot of stimuli around you. It is ideal to just mind your own business and stop worrying about other people or things around you.

Here are some tips to help you mind your own business:

1. **Take Responsibility For Yourself**

    Taking responsibility for yourself means that you know that no one can make you do something or feel anything aside from yourself. You should not let anyone else have authority over you. You always have an option. Minding your own business is choosing not to be controlled and taking ownership of yourself and your decisions. For example, you are not required to work or do your taxes. You just choose to do those things because you want the results and you do not want to deal with the consequences of not doing them.

Taking responsibility is telling yourself that you went to work on a Sunday because you want to get a promotion or you want to get an extra salary instead of telling yourself that your boss made you come to work. Of course, you should not act outside of your integrity, be narcissistic, or treat others poorly. After all, we live in a society that has certain agreements that we made with each other to help things work out fine.

In the end, you are free to break social expectations, do whatever it is that you want, and act however you want because we all have free will. You are just not free from the consequences of your actions and decisions.

2. Accept Other People As They Are

Accepting other people as they are means that you accept the person fully, including their flaws and imperfections. However, this does not mean that you should allow other people's destructive behavior without saying anything or doing anything to prevent it. It does not mean that you should not set boundaries for yourself or that you should not make someone in your family that is addicted to illegal drugs take therapy or you do not discipline your child when they do something that is not correct.

When we do not accept others for who they are, we are subconsciously telling them that we do not want them to be who they are and we want them to act or be in a certain way that we want. We should accept people even if they are sometimes late to an appointment, they normally talk louder than you want them to be, they like some things that we think arc boring, do things that we do not agree with, or believe in something that we do not believe in. We should accept that reality, respect them, and love them for who they are.

3. Listen To Other People Without Judging or Trying To Control Them

When someone talks about their problem with you, always keep in mind that you do not always have to tell them what to do. Your main role is to just listen and understand their situation. No one is broken and you do not have to fix anyone. When you are listening to someone who is speaking to you, instead of judging or criticizing them, you should think about how you can learn from their situation or how their situation applies to you. Think about how you would feel and react if you were in their shoes. After all, every human experience is universal. We are all connected, what is happening to others right now can also happen to you in the future or it has already happened to you before. And judging others is not going to help anyone, it will just create negativity. When someone tells you their problem, listen to them and try to understand what they are going through instead of thinking that they are in need of help and you should help them. You should only offer your help and you should never force it on them. If the other person thinks that they need your help, they will accept your help and be grateful for it.

4. Do Not Believe Every Thought In Your Head

When you mind your own business, you can save a lot of energy because you will only need to focus on what you want instead of the things that you do not want. It is like sorting your email. You can think of your mind like it is your email inbox and the thoughts that you are having are the emails that you receive.

Think about all the time and energy that you need to spend to go through every email that you receive. Some are special offers and promotions, important emails about work, personal messages from someone who is close to you, or spam emails that are just a waste of your time. It would take you all day to sort out everything one by one. Instead, what most of us do is that we just take a quick glance each day and try to see what actually needs our time and attention, after that we delete the rest of it.

Thoughts are just like that, we can think about something all day and they would not be important or would not necessarily be helpful. Part of minding our own business is figuring out which of our thoughts are true, important, and useful instead of wasting our time thinking about every thought that crosses our minds.

This would also be the case with our feelings and emotions. Some of them are brief and do not require much of our attention while others can be relevant and you need to pay close attention to them. Always remember that while our feelings are often relevant and helpful, they are not always trustworthy. They might be based on a reality that is not true or they are not legitimate for your current situation. Ask yourself whether your thoughts and feelings are true, important, and useful or whether they are just noises in our heads that we need to ignore.

5. **Practice Self-awareness**

Minding your own business is about being self-observant. It is about observing what is going on inside your mind and what it is that you are doing. It can be helpful to think of yourself as two people, the one that thinks and does the action while the other one is the observer that watches over the first one. You can observe yourself, your actions, and whatever you are thinking about. You will be your own observer.

When you think of something, you can automatically believe what you are thinking or your observer self can watch your thought and say "Is that really true or you just want to believe that because it is convenient for you?". You do not have to believe everything that you might think about. Most of your thoughts are not even correct because you do not always know both sides of the story or you might just be carried away by your emotions in the heat of the moment.

For example, when someone is walking in front of you and you cannot overtake them, you might think to yourself that the person in front of you is walking too slowly and is trying to block you on purpose. Your observer self can notice this and make a counter-argument saying "I am making a judgment. Is that judgment really true? Are they really walking too slowly or are they just walking at a pace that they are comfortable with? I should not decide on how fast other people should walk. Maybe I am just walking too fast and I am being impatient." You might even notice that your thoughts are absurd and you are just overreacting. Observe and acknowledge the fact that you are thinking those thoughts then you can move on and know that those thoughts could just be like spam mail in the inbox of your mind and you do not have to open them and instead, you can ignore them and move them straight to your trash inbox.

Learn To See The Bigger Picture

Big picture thinking is the ability to understand abstract concepts, possibilities, and ideas. Big picture thinkers emphasize the whole system of operation they are working on. Think of it like when you are crossing the road, you not only look to one side of the road right? Instead, look to your left if there are any vehicles passing the road, then you look to your right, and you also look ahead in front of you on where you are about to walk. That is essentially what big picture thinking is, looking at the entirety of a situation or a plan.

Learning to see the bigger picture will help you avoid overthinking about every small detail that can bother you when you have hypersensitivity. It will also be less likely that you will fret over the details that would not matter in the long run. And also, being able to see the bigger picture, you will most likely see how an obstacle can affect the whole situation and how you can turn that obstacle into a stepping stone for a better life.

Here are some ways to help you line up your brain to see the bigger picture:

1. **Eliminate The Habits That Prevents You From Seeing The Bigger Picture**

   Some of our natural way of thinking can prevent us from seeing the bigger picture, so the first step is to break the bad habits that prevent you from being able to see the bigger picture. One of these bad habits is being too much of a perfectionist that you sweat over all the small kinds of things. If you are always looking for something to change to make them better, scrambling to reach perfection and nothing is good enough for you. You will be more focused on some of the small details that do not even matter in the long run. Maybe you are spending too much time thinking about where you will place the new plant pot that you bought. You need to stop yourself, take a break, have a step back, and look for wider opportunities to help the overall situation instead of focusing on perfecting every small detail.

2. **Set Aside Some Time To Help You Think**

   This might be an obvious tip but it is actually baffling how much we forgot about setting aside some time to help us think. Everyone is in a rush these days, trying to make a decision in the shortest amount of time possible. If you are just doing what is the next item on your list without taking a break, you will never be able to have time to think about the bigger picture, there will always be something that feels more urgent even though they can be delayed even if just a little bit. Set aside some time to think when you feel like you are the most creative. Your brain may feel the clearest a few hours after you have just woken up or at night when your surroundings are quiet and calm. Do what you think is best for you.

3. Learn To Pick Specific Goals

Dividing your big picture thinking into a few specific goals will make them much more doable. If you want to renovate your house, break down this goal into more specific actions that have a set deadline. For example, in the next few weeks, you may want to think about what parts you want to be renovated. Then after that, you can think about the new theme you want to do.

Big questions are worthwhile to ask as long as they are not overwhelming and they should be formulated in a way that does not feel burdensome or insurmountable. If that is the case, divide them into smaller pieces that will make them feel like they are doable. Identify the problem and think of several solutions for it so that if the first solution did not succeed, you still have another plan.

4. Identify The Steps That You Are Able To Take Actions Upon

When we have a big goal, chances are, you will generally procrastinate on doing it unless you find a way of starting it. Finding out where to start is usually the hardest part of doing something. If what you are doing is something that you have done before, you can think about the steps that you did earlier. But if it is something new, you should ask for guidance from someone who has done it before. Being able to see the bigger picture not only means that you see and understand the whole situation, but you should also see and understand each of the components that are acting on the whole situation. Take a look at them one by one and determine which one you should be doing first and everything else will most likely follow through their respective places.

Choose Your Battles Wisely

1. Try To Assess The Problem

Whether you believe it or not, most of the problems that we tackle in our day-to-day lives are small, petty things that do not have an impact in the long run. This includes negative people who try to contaminate you with their negativity. When faced with a problem, you might want to ask yourself if that problem is really important if you really need to deal with it, or can your time be better spent elsewhere.

For example, when someone who you thought is your friend said something bad about you in your workplace. You would think that this person is bad and what he did is unfriendly. If you would really think about it, you can just move on with it and just cut ties with the person involved straight away without worrying too much about it. You should realize that you have plenty of other things to worry about in your life and it is not worth it for you to waste your time and mental energy on someone who is already making you suffer throughout the course of your friendship.

Similarly, you may also experience coming across someone who is a narcissist and will keep on bragging about himself and will insult you nonstop. He will insult everything about you and will give you unwanted remarks. And if he does this to you, again and again, then you should realize that it is pointless for you to refute his statements and pick a fight with him because his comments came from his inferiority complex and are not the truth. Instead, you should also cut ties with this person immediately to prevent any more similar incidents.

If you have a problem, think about how we all only have 24 hours each day and only a few hours of that can be spent on being productive. How would you want to spend your precious time? Do you want to keep being angry about someone who is not worth your time or on the petty things that will not matter a couple of years from now? Or, do you want to be spending your time cultivating yourself and helping yourself grow towards a better life? It is your choice to make and I believe that you already know what the correct answer is.

2. Weigh The Pros And Cons

When you need to face an upcoming battle, considering the pros and cons of that battle will help you decide if it is a battle worth fighting. You should ask yourself whether the cons of that battle outweigh its pros, if the answer is yes, then it will generally be beneficial for you to just let go of the problem and move on. You should also ask yourself about your odds of success, if the odds of success are extremely low, then it will be better for you to just let go of the problem and move on as well.

For example, imagine a scenario when you are given a job to produce a product. You did everything you can to make this product, you dedicated all your time and attention to that work while also disregarding all the other projects you have to focus on producing the product. After all your hard work, the product is made and it received good feedback from the customers that bought it. However, even though the company is supposed to market the product, they eventually stopped supporting the product without informing you. You then decided to follow up about this matter multiple times but the company only promised to do something but they never did anything. The contractual clauses that you signed when the company gave you this project are going to relinquish your selling rights, and given that the company is supposed to market the product that you made but backed out on the arrangement, it will put you in a losing deal because you had already spent all your time and energy into creating that high-quality product but you cannot even sell it yourself.

This will surely make you feel very angry at this point but it is advisable to not pursue the matter any further. The reason is that the company already went out of touch even though the subsequent attempts you have done to follow up. Even though the company is at fault in this scenario, there will be little to nothing for you to gain in pursuing this matter any further. The company already stopped contacting you which meant any further attempt to communicate is going to be more difficult. And also, even if you had your way with that company and reinstated marketing support, you will only gain a little increase in your revenue. It would be easier to achieve that goal by launching another product rather than forcing a response from a company that is already ignoring you.

Does this mean that you should keep away from all the battles that have little to no chance of success? No, not at all. Sometimes you would want to pick a battle to make a statement. For example, when there is a case of sexual harassment in your office, medical negligence in a hospital, or bullying in school, you should raise these kinds of issues and let others know about the problem. The reward that you get from engaging in a battle does not always have to be monetary, it can also be a moral reward, like protecting our rights or preventing the problem from ever happening again. Every situation is different so weigh the pros and cons of a problem before you decide on what you will do next.

3. Try To Go For A Win-win Scenario Instead Of A Win-lose

If you ever decide to pick a battle, you should try to go for a win-win scenario. Work towards an outcome that would make both parties benefit from the situation as much as possible. You may be surprised by that suggestion and ask yourself "Why should I go for a win-win scenario instead of a win-lose scenario? Why would I want to help my opponent also win?"

Even though we are using the word battle as an analogy for when we are facing a problem, you should also consider your opponent as your ally or a friend. The reason for this is simple, if you have the mindset to crush other people and you always need to have a winner and a loser in every scenario, we would end up with a world where there is a shortage of opportunities for everyone because someone would have to lose every time.

While this mindset is pretty common because of the hyper-competitiveness of our day to day lives. If you are thinking this way, it would only end up with you being boxed into limitations. We have unlimited opportunities in the world, we just have to find these opportunities or help create them. When you focus your mindset on a win-win scenario for everyone, you attract an abundance of opportunities. You will also share love and positivity with everyone.

The battle is not about fighting against your opponent, you should focus on fighting the conflict instead. If you are frustrated with a colleague, talk to him and find a way to help you both match your needs and wants. If you are having problems with your significant other, do not try to make things more complicated by using passive-aggressive methods towards him. You should talk to him and work out your differences, this way, you will be able to achieve both of your goals together. If you are angry with your friend but you do not want your friendship with them to end, talk to them and let them know your struggles that you are dealing with that are related to your friendship. Take on this win-win scenario mindset for every problem that you face with anyone. Ask yourself what is the scenario that will make everyone happy and that will make everyone win, then do your best to work towards that outcome.

4. Have An Open Discussion With The Other Person

An important part of getting the win-win scenario that we are aiming for is to have an open discussion with the other person you are having problems with. When we act based on only what we can see, we are shutting down the other person without listening to what they have to say. We should respect that the other person also has their views and goals that may be different from our own views and goals. To achieve a win-win scenario, we should listen to what they have to say and discuss the best outcome for all of the parties involved.

Let me tell you a story about my significant other. There was a time when I have been feeling a hidden resentment about him and I felt like I have been giving too much of my time to my family: working at my job, taking care of our kids, and doing all the house chores. I feel like I am putting my ideal life on hold because I am spending too much time taking care of our family and my significant other is not doing much to help me. I still love my significant others and we are still affectionate with each other even though we have been married for a long time already. This was simply an issue that has only been going on for a little while.

I decided to talk to my significant other about this issue and we had a very in-depth discussion in a way that we do not usually have. My significant other was surprised to learn about the way I am feeling and reaffirmed his support and care for me. We reached an agreement and said that we will find more ways to earn money and share the household responsibilities among ourselves rather than letting only one of us take all the burden. This brought us closer to each other even more.

On the other hand, if my significant other and I did not have that open discussion, perhaps things would have been worse and I might have acted in a passive-aggressive manner like picking fights and being argumentative with proper reason. That would have created more conflicts and would have made my significant other unhappy just like me. It would make our household suffer and be filled with negativity for everyone in the house. My significant other would still be clueless about how I am feeling and what is going on, and the original conflict would not be resolved. In that scenario, it is not just me who is losing but every one of us.

Here are a few small tips to help you have an open discussion with someone:

- Try to understand the other person. Every one of us has different views and opinions, and you want to understand what the other person's views are. Do not dismiss their views just because you have a different opinion from them. Understand how the other person feels, why they are acting the way they are, what they are thinking, and why they think that way.

- Share your side and also let the other person have the chance to share their side. Work on the differences that you have by sharing your thoughts. Then invite the other person to also share their thoughts with you. Make sure that you both have an equal amount of chance to share your opinions, ask questions you have for each other, and understand each other in the process.

- Be supportive. While the other person is sharing their opinion, you should nod, acknowledge what they are saying and thank them for sharing their side. This would make them comfortable to share their side with you and make them feel that you are willing to listen to them.

- Brainstorm the best solution that would benefit all of the parties involved. Make sure that you make it clear to them that you care about the other person and you want to make a scenario where everyone would benefit in the end. Work together with them and try to think of a solution given both of your needs.

5. **Try To Keep Your Cool**

Once you have decided to fight a battle, try to keep yourself calm and collected to achieve the best outcome for everyone. Remember that your goal is to have a win-win situation and not to bring the other person down. Your true enemy is the conflict at hand and not the other person.

However, when we are faced with a conflict, it may be hard for us to remain calm and to think carefully. Sometimes, our emotions can get to us and we may say something that we do not mean in the heat of the situation. An unaired grievance may open up. You may feel like attacking the other person verbally, even if you know in yourself that it is not the goal. You may also feel like running away from the battle if the other person is not being cooperative with you. Here are some tips to help you manage this kind of situation:

- Before facing your problems, you should meditate. Imagine that you are in a calm and tranquil place. No one can take away this place from you and no one will be able to hurt you in there unless you let them do it.

- If someone told you anything hurtful, try to think calmly and approach it in a peaceful way. Say that you understand that they are angry and you want to keep the situation as peaceful as possible. Also, tell them that you want to achieve the best outcome that will benefit both of you and invite them to work together with you to make things right.

- If you are feeling that you are losing your cool, take a step back and calm yourself, stop talking and try to compose yourself. Imagine that you are in a different place away from the things that make you angry. You are there to carry out the discussion peacefully and nothing can stop that unless you let them.

6. Have An Exit Point

All battles can be won if you have unlimited resources but that is just not possible. The reality is that we can never have unlimited resources. We cannot spend our time forever solving a problem that is not progressing even just a little bit despite giving it our best efforts. You should have a point where it tells you that it is enough and it is time to cut your losses. This is the point to exit the battle because you have already suffered enough losses because of this battle and you do not want to invest any more time or effort into this problem because it will not improve the situation anymore.

One of my friends who travels a lot had an incident where he and his wife got scammed into paying more than they should for a taxi ride. The taxi driver made use of the fact that it is their first time there and they are not familiar with the local currency and he lied to my friends about the bill. The driver even smiled at them happily while he took the money from them. It is not that much money in general but it is more about the dishonesty rather than the amount of money that is lost. It was their honeymoon and they felt irritated that they met a dishonest person at a celebratory event. The hotel staff was friendly and helped them try to track down the taxi driver. They reviewed the CCTV footage of the incident and tried calling the driver but they could not reach him through the phone.

After an hour of trying to solve the issue, my friend decided to let go of the problem since there was no way to locate the driver because the CCTV footage is too blurry and they cannot recognize the driver, and the driver was unlikely to admit what he did to my friends even if they are able to contact the taxi company that the driver is working for. Moreover, the amount is not really huge money and it would be easier for them to earn it back rather than spending a lot of time trying to get it back from the taxi driver.

They enjoyed the rest of their trip after letting go of the incident because it is a draining situation that is hard to deal with. Maybe they could have found the driver if they had requested for a zoom-in analysis of the CCTV footage, but the success of that is very low and it would take a lot of time and effort. It was easier to just let it go and focus on the bigger things.

7. Learn To Let Go Of The Problem If It Remains Unsolved

If the problem remains unsolved despite giving it your best efforts, let it go. Success does not come from winning every battle, it comes from knowing when to fight a certain battle and knowing when it is time to let things go. While the previous tip is about knowing when to exit when things go your way, this tip is about letting go. Just because you stop fighting a battle does not mean you have let go of it mentally, it can still be bothering you in your mind.

There was a friend of mine that was having issues with her boss and colleagues. They kept backstabbing her, talking behind her back, and giving her lots of problems. Their office was cliquish and she did not fit in very well.

She felt deeply troubled and she even cried at her office at one point, after that she realized that she had enough. She decided to focus on her goals and the next step towards progressing her career. She worked on her resume and started applying for a new job. After a while, she found a new job that has better pay and better working conditions. She has since been working there for a few years and is enjoying her work and her coworkers. If she had focused on feeling unhappy about her previous workplace and being angry at her coworkers, she would never have the chance to find her current job that is way better.

So, how can you really let go? Here are some tips to help you with letting go of the problems that you should not be bothered with:

- Acknowledge your feelings and emotions. Something went wrong and things did not go the way you wanted them to be, how would that make you feel? Are you going to feel sad? Disappointed? Or angry? Write down your feelings and acknowledge them. Know that your feelings are real and they are valid. Do not run away from and let yourself feel how you are feeling, do not suppress your feelings just because they are not happy feelings.

- After acknowledging your feelings and emotions, try to understand why you are feeling that way. I know for a fact that surely, there is a reason why you are feeling aggrieved. Why are you feeling this way? What made you feel that the situation is unfair? Try to dig down and find the root of the issue. Maybe you feel that they are disrespecting you, maybe the situation confronts one of your deepest fears, or maybe it deals with something that is very important to you. Uncovering the cause of the issue will help you understand and let go of the problem.

- Start working on a new path forward. Since the problem cannot be resolved to your desired outcome, try to think about what you can do to move forward. Identify new ways to move forward. My friend could not figure out a way to resolve the conflict involving her boss and her coworkers being mean to her, therefore, her next step to move forward is to look for a new job and it worked out great for her. So, think about how you can stay on track with your life goals despite the fact that the battle did not turn out the way you wanted it to be.

Separate The Person From The Issue

When facing a problem, it is important for all the parties involved to tackle the problem and not attack each other. The goal is to go easy on the other person and go hard on the problem at hand. Failing to interact with the other person sensitively can be harmful to building or maintaining a working relationship. Knowing the other party personally can help build a cordial relationship between both parties involved. Find a way to know more about the person so that you can separate them from the issue. There are three categories in which you can identify and address people-related problems to solve the issue with an opposing party's perception, emotion, and communication.

1. **Perception**

   The biggest hurdle that you can face while trying to solve a problem can often be found in your head. To solve a problem, you must first understand why the problem began and what the perception of the other person is. To understand how another person thinks, you must first understand the depth and power of their perception. Understanding the other party's side can help to open the path to a good solution to your conflict. This will help you build a foundation for communication to allow you to find opportunities on how to react consistently to the other person's negative perception. You should be a good listener and understand the other person.

2. Emotion

Conflicts can bring out the worst in everyone and emotions often run rampant. Emotions are real and very powerful, and if left unchecked, can be a huge hindrance in solving a problem. For example, anger and fear are both genuine and commanding emotions, even if they are ill-founded. Those emotions need to be addressed first before attempting reconciliation. Before starting to face your problem, try to recognize and acknowledge that the other person's emotions are also legitimate just like your emotions, and do not be dismissive. Just because something is less important for you does not mean that it is not very important for them. It will almost be impossible to negotiate if one of the sides is being disrespectful. If needed, allow the other person to blow off steam and let them calm down first. You should also remember to not react emotionally. You can vent out your emotions to other people if that will help you.

3. Communication

Many people will tell you that the key to every relationship is communication and comprehension. It is also very important when you are solving a problem. Resolving an issue requires both parties to listen and to share their opinion in an attempt to come to an understanding. The steps for communicating the correct way, even though it is very basic, are extremely important.

The first thing you need to do is to pay very close attention to the person speaking and take note of what is said and what is not said. The next thing to do is to acknowledge the things that are said and do not assume something that is not said, it is okay to ask for you to verify your thoughts so you do not assume something and later it turns out that it is wrong. After that, you should paraphrase your understanding of the other person's statement to make sure that you understand what they said correctly and that you are both on the same page. Ask the other person to clarify something if you did not understand it in their statement. This does not mean that you should always have to agree on what they said, it just means that you should know and understand what they believe in and how they are feeling about it. As we said before, it is important to make sure you understand their perception.

When it is your turn to speak, speak with a purpose to try to really solve the issue person to person. In order to communicate in a constructive way, you should speak about yourself and not about the other person. Tell them about how you feel and what you think about the situation. It is hard to challenge a statement about yourself. Do not blame the other person for the problem that is happening because they will get defensive and the communication will break down or it will be shifted away from the main issue. That will make it hard for both of you to resolve the problem. Make sure to remember that the enemy is not the other person but the problem that you are both facing. You are not fighting against each other, you are both fighting to solve the same problem that you are both in.

Ask For Help

Every one of us needs help, especially if we are hypersensitive. It may not be easy to ask for help because of the fear of looking stupid or incapable but this self-handicapping mindset might be the biggest thing that is holding you back. It may provide you comfort for a short time but this will often be a hindrance to your development in the long run. Asking for help can also benefit the person who will try to help you and everyone around you. Here are more reasons why you should ask for help:

1. **Asking For Help Develops Relationship**

    When you are asking for help or when you are sharing your personal information and problems with other people, it demonstrates to the other person that you like them and you are willing to develop a relationship. By sharing your personal information, you will be able to create a positive impression of yourself to the other person. People who are willing to share their personal information are seen as people who are more trusting, friendly, and trustworthy. These are the things that everyone is looking for when they are choosing who to develop a relationship with.

2. **Asking For Help Is A Sign Of A High Performer**

    It was found that high-performing individuals are more likely to ask advice from their colleagues. This may be because the high performers want to improve and be better, so they seek advice to help themselves identify their weaknesses and work on them. A second possible explanation could be that low-performing individuals are less likely to seek advice because they believe that their performance level is already high and they do not need to improve, so they are stuck in performing poorly.

3. **Asking For Help Improves Resilience**

    Asking for help will allow you to surround yourself with good people who can make you feel positive energies and will help you to facilitate further development for yourself. These people will create optimism and hope that will help you be able to deal with challenging situations which will improve your resilience. If you are able to ask for help and obtain positive feedback from others, you can overcome setbacks and be able to grow, which are the key traits you need to enhance your resilience.

4. Asking For Help Develops Growth Mindset

Help from others can be obtained in the form of praise and feedback, which can help you improve your performance. It is found out that children who were praised for their intelligence were more likely to choose tasks that made them look more intelligent in the future. However, children who were praised for their hard work were more likely to choose tasks that would allow them to learn new information and improve themselves. This means that if you are asking for help and someone appreciates your efforts, it will make you confident with your hard work and would make you want to improve yourself even more.

5. Asking For Help Improves Your Mental Health

The key to improving your mental health is the feeling of being connected to others and learning new things in life. Both of these things can be developed when you are asking others for help. When you are alone and you isolate yourself from other people, it will often lead to you being more worried, doubting yourself, and it will bring lots of stress to your mind. We have a saying that says "No man is an island" and that is true, humanity survived because we stuck together and helped each other out.

6. Asking For Help Is Viewed By Others As A Good Character Trait

We often believe that other people see our vulnerability as a sign of weakness, but the truth is almost the exact opposite. Others think of our ability to share our weaknesses and vulnerability as a sign of courage. It is not easy and it takes courage to show that you are vulnerable and you have weaknesses. People often perceive their own vulnerability in a much more negative manner while they think of the ones shown by others in a less negative way.

7. A Team Is Often Better Than One Individual

Having a team around you is better than only dealing with the problem with just yourself because it enhances effort levels. Being surrounded by hard-working people will also help you increase your work ethic too. But what is even more interesting is that this effect was found regardless of the fact that whether the said individual was doing an easier or harder task than you or whether the task was similar or unrelated to what you are doing. It will still improve yourself and you can all solve a problem easier if you have someone to help you.

We have established that asking for help is beneficial not just for you but also for the people who are going to help you and for everyone that is around both parties. You should also know how to ask for help properly and how to get people to help you in a good manner. Here are the things that you need to do while asking for help to actually get other people to help you:

1. **Show That You Respect Them**

    When you are asking for help, you should always show respect to the person you are asking. No one is going to help someone who is rude and is being arrogant. Be humble and respect the person that you are trying to ask for help.

2. **Show That You Trust Them**

    You are vulnerable and you admit that you have weaknesses. Show the other person that you trust them with that knowledge. You trust that they will not take advantage of your weakness and vulnerabilities. You should say it to them and show them that you trust them to make them comfortable and trust you too.

3. Show That You Are Willing To Listen To Them

When you ask for help, instead of ordering around the other person and telling them exactly how they should help you, you should give them the freedom to decide on how they can help. You should not ask them to tell you what you want to hear and they should say what they think you should do instead. If they have the option to do what they can to help you, they will be more likely to help you.

4. Be Grateful For The Help That Is Given To You

After someone has helped you, you should always be thankful and show your appreciation to the person that helped you. When someone agrees to help you, you should always say thank you. If it is appropriate, you can consider ways to either celebrate or reward the help that is given to you.

Have A Sense of Humor

Having a sense of humor is good for your well-being. You can think of your sense of humor as the immune system of your mind. People that are at risk of depression tend to fall into depressive episodes when they are exposed to negative things and afterward, it becomes easier and easier for them to relapse into depression. However, reframing negative events in a humorous light acts as a kind of emotional filter to help them prevent the negativity from triggering a depressive episode.

Humor does not just guard you against depression, it will also improve your overall quality of life. Researchers have found that people who scored higher on certain types of humor tests have better confidence, have greater self-competence, have more control over their anxiety, and have a better overall performance in social interactions. However, not all kinds of humor are the same. There are four types of humor:

1. **Affiliative Humor**

   This is the type of humor that is designed to strengthen social bonds. It involves telling jokes about things that everyone might find funny. The goal of this humor is to bring people together to find the fun in our day-to-day lives. The types of jokes that this humor represents are the ones that focus on comedy in our daily lives. The goal is to create a sense of friendship, kindness, happiness, and well-being for everybody. If you like jokes about animals and everyday occurrences, then you might have an affiliative sense of humor.

2. **Self-enhancing Humor**

   This type of humor is related to having a good-natured attitude towards your life. It is about telling jokes that you are able to laugh about yourself, such as making a joke when something bad has happened to you but in a non-detrimental manner. If you try to find humor in everyday situations and make yourself the target of the humor in a good-natured way, then you might have this type of humor. This type of humor is related to healthy coping with stressful situations.

3. **Aggressive Humor**

This is the type of humor that involves putting others down or insulting a target individual. When your jokes are intended to threaten or hurt someone psychologically, then it is the type of humor used by bullies. Aggressive humor often disregards the effect it might have on others. While some others will find this type of humor funny, others might just laugh to cover up the feeling of discomfort that they are having. It is when you are laughing at the expense of others.

4. **Self-defeating Humor**

This is the type of humor where you put yourself down in an aggressive fashion in order to gain approval from others. It is making others laugh at the expense of yourself. Psychologically speaking, this type of humor can be an unhealthy form of humor and is sometimes used by targets of bullies to try to avoid being bullied, they make themselves the butt of the joke before others can put them down and ridicule them.

The positive effects that we mentioned earlier are only seen with individuals who scored highly in affiliative humor and self-enhancing humor, while aggressive humor and self-defeating humor were associated with poorer overall well-being and higher anxiety or depression. So, if you want to cultivate your sense of humor, it is important to aim for the right kind of humor that will benefit you and the people around you. Here are some tips to help you improve your sense of humor:

1. **Recognize The Difference Between Having A Sense Of Humor And Just Being Funny**

   Being funny means that you are able to express your humor, like telling a funny story, a well-timed joke, or a witty pun. Having a sense of humor means that you have the ability to let go of the little things that you should not be bothered by and not taking things very seriously, and be able to laugh at it instead or at least see the humor in life's absurdities.

2. **Try To Find Your Funny Bone And Learn From Others**

   Try to think about what things make you laugh or what things that make you smile and lighten up your mood. This is a good way to start improving your sense of humor. If you are not sure about what things make you laugh, you can observe other people and learn from them. How do the people around you, like your friends and family, laugh at the world around them and the things that are happening to them? Take note that you should be careful while observing other people because you might just copy their humor. True humor is genuine and it should reflect your personality.

3. Focus More On Having Fun Instead Of Just Being Funny

Having a sense of humor will help you have fun even though life is throwing you problems or any other negativity. That means that you can laugh at life and poke fun at your situation instead of just feeling sad and down. Always remember that your focus is to have fun more often.

4. Find The Humor In Commonalities

People tend to laugh more often at jokes that deal with their current situations, where they live, or what they believe in. People laugh at something that they can relate to. Make a light joke about the weather or the city you live in to start a conversation with other people. If you happen to be in the same business, you can make a joke about your current profession.

5. Surround Yourself With Other Funny People

Think about the funny people around you, your funny friends or relatives, how they slip humor into their conversations, and what kind of jokes they make? Check out other comedians and focus on their delivery, topics, and how they turn their day-to-day lives into something funny. Take a look at the people in your life that you consider funny and find out what it is that you like about their humor and what you can add to your own. Being surrounded by other funny people will also help you improve your humor and make you funnier.

6. Be Careful Not To Hurt Other People's Feelings

Whether you are telling jokes or laughing at them, you want to be careful so that you do not offend anyone or hurt their feelings. Having a good sense of humor means you approach life with a good-natured attitude. You should not use others to get a laugh and you should not laugh when other people are making fun of others. If you are telling a joke, think about its context. Is the joke appropriate for work, home, a date, or the people you are with? Or will it offend someone? Think about it carefully and be sure to avoid jokes that will hurt other people's feelings.

7. Look On The Bright Side Of Life And Learn To Laugh

Looking on the bright side of life and learning to laugh is the key to a good sense of humor. You should focus on laughing more often every day, even laughing at yourself or the situation you are in. Enjoy the little things in life, find humor in every situation you can, and try to find humor in your life's misfortunes. Smile as often as you can. Try making other people laugh too. Make laughing a priority not just for yourself but also for other people.

8. Laugh Instead Of Reacting And Let Go Of Your Defensiveness

When you find yourself in a tense situation, step back and try to laugh instead. Anger is a powerful emotion but laughter is also powerful and it has a strong hold over our minds and bodies. Tell a short joke and laugh at the situation or use humor to defuse the anger that you are feeling about the situation. It might save you some stress and heartache. Let go of things that make you feel defensive. Forget about all the judgments, criticism, and self-doubts that you feel. Instead, let those bothersome feelings get off your back as you have a sense of humor and laugh about them. No one is out to criticize you or to get you, you should always smile and laugh instead.

9. Accept Yourself And Be Spontaneous

Having a light-hearted attitude about yourself is one of the ways to keep a sense of humor. Learn to accept yourself and laugh at yourself. Of course, you also need to take yourself seriously from time to time, but learning to laugh at yourself is also a way to learn to accept yourself. All of us have imperfections and no one is perfect, every one of us makes mistakes. Do not be too hard on yourself and keep good humor about your life. Laugh off the things you cannot control. Even if you feel uncomfortable in making fun of yourself, shrug that stuff off especially if it is something that you cannot change. Once you accept yourself, you should also be spontaneous. Most people would not do something because they are afraid that it might make them look silly or they might be scared of failing. Having a good sense of humor about yourself can help you get over the things that are holding you back. A sense of humor helps you get out of your comfort zone and helps you let go of all your inhibitions so that you can experience your life to the fullest, no matter if your endeavors become successful or not.

How To Stop Negative Energy And Stress

As a psychic empath, you will be more vulnerable to negative energies and stress because of your highly sensitive perception. You might absorb the stress of other people and the negative energies around you even if you do not want to. This is because of your ability to sense and feel their stress and emotions. When you sense negative energy or stress, you are going to absorb it because of your psychic ability. To prevent negative energy and stress from getting to you,

you should avoid or spend less time with the person or environment that is causing the stress and negative energies as much as possible.

Empaths Naturally Struggle With The Following Situations

Due to the innate ability of a psychic empath to sense and absorb the negative energies and emotions of other people, it is important to know what situations can make a psychic empath struggle and what you can do in these situations to help you handle them.

1. **Handling Stress**

   Stress is a natural reaction we feel when we feel anxious or threatened. Learning to handle your stress is important for a psychic empath because stress can affect them more than a normal person. It is because of the fact that they are more sensitive to stimulations and because they can sense and absorb the stress of other people. Getting the right care and support will help anyone reduce stressful feelings and symptoms. Here are some healthy ways to handle your stress:

   - Take care of yourself more often. You should eat healthy foods, exercise regularly, get plenty of sleep, and give yourself a break from time to time especially if you feel stressed out.

   - Talk to other people. Share your problems and how you are feeling to a close friend or family member that you know will not judge you. Being able to vent out your feelings to someone can help you feel better about them. Your close friend or family member can also give you advice on how to deal with your problem.

- Avoid drugs and alcohol. Taking drugs and alcohol may create the illusion of you forgetting about your problem but the problem is still there and they can even create additional problems for you and increase the stress that you are already feeling.

- Take a break and rest. If watching news of current events on the television is causing you stress, take a break from watching the news. Take a rest and meditate to be calm and lessen your stress.

- Acknowledge it when you need more help. If your problems are getting persistent and you are thinking about harming yourself, talk to a professional who can help you like a psychologist, a social worker, or a professional counselor.

2. Protecting Yourself From Narcissists And Other Negative Energy

Narcissistic people produce a lot of negative energy that is harmful to a psychic empath's well-being. Most of us know or have been involved with a narcissist. They may be a family member, an officemate, or one of the members of your social group. It may be hard to avoid them because they are naturally drawn to a psychic empath's positive energy but here are some tips to help you protect yourself from narcissistic people and other negative energies:

- Ignore the narcissistic people. Like when you are dealing with a bully in school, if you ignore them, it gives them no satisfaction and they will find someone else to bother.

- Do not take the bait and fight with them. Turn the other way and do not just defend or justify your actions to them when you do.

- Understand their criticism for what it is, it is not about you. Their behavior is because of the fact that they have a disorder. Do not take what is said to you personally. It is most likely just a reflection of their insecurities.

- When you communicate, set a clear boundary and use clear communication. Tell them how you feel and say it directly.

- If you choose to make a decision to stay away from them, let them know it and make it clear and bold. You also need to make sure that you follow through with your decision to stay away from them and do not be discouraged.

- Believe in your own intuition and feelings. Our bodies and minds tell us when something is not right and when people are treating us badly. Follow your intuitions and avoid that person.

- Remember that you have the chance to protect yourself from them and you can do it. Do not just expect other people to rescue you from a narcissist or any other bad situation. It will be an empowering experience if you stand up for yourself and you let your voice be heard.

- Remember that every one of us deserves to be treated with kindness and compassion, and that also includes you. It is a worthwhile goal to work hard to bring more kindness into our world for everyone. Be an example for your kids, friends, family, and everyone around you.

3. Become Aware Of Your Feeling

Psychic empaths can be confused about what they are feeling because sometimes they might think that what they are feeling is their own feelings but instead, it is the feelings of someone around them and they are just sensing the other person's feelings. Here are some tips to help you differentiate what you are feeling and the feelings of others that you are sensing.

- Notice what kind of emotion you are having and try to think about what is the cause of it. If you are feeling sad because something bad happened or you have received a piece of bad news, then that is surely your own emotion that you feel but if you are feeling sad and there is nothing wrong that happened, it might just be the feeling of someone around and you are mirroring it because of your psychic empath ability to sense other people's emotions.

- You should broaden your emotional vocabulary. Our words are extremely important. If you are experiencing a strong emotion, take a moment to consider what to call it. Once you have identified it, you can also try to come up with two or more words that describe how you are feeling specifically. This way you can unearth a deeper emotion buried beneath the more obvious one. It is important to do this with both positive emotions and negative emotions. Being able to say that you are excited about your new job and not just nervous or that you trust a colleague instead of just thinking that he is nice for example, will help you set your intentions for the role or the relationship in a way that is more specific and more likely to be clear for you and for everyone to understand.

- Talk about your feelings with other people or write them down in a journal. Discussing your feelings with other people can greatly benefit you. It can give you a sense of control over yourself, provide you with a deeper perspective, reduce the impact of stress, and can help you determine the feelings that you are having. Talking about your feelings out loud with a close friend, family member, or even when you are alone will not only help you see things differently, it also gives you time to focus more and use logic to think carefully. This will lead to you reducing your feelings of threat and anxiety, you can rationalize the events, and your emotions will normalize. You will recognize that the feelings you have are normal and are also faced by other people.

4. Ridding Yourself Of Excess Energy

Getting rid of excess energy can be hard for a psychic empath because there is too much energy getting absorbed into their mind and body all at once and it can be overwhelming. Having excess energy can make you feel like you cannot sleep, you feel endlessly fidgety, and make you lack focus or motivation and you will get nothing done. There are many ways that energy can get stuck within us and if wc do not have an outlet or we are unable to process the energy quickly enough. Here are a few causes of excess energy and how you can deal with it:

- Fear and Anxiety for a psychic empath are incredibly overwhelming because of his hypersensitivity. As a person who can sense the environment or what is coming to us without leaving the house, when we feel threatened, our psychic ability becomes more sensitive to sense threats. It literally puts your spiritual and physical senses into overdrive. This means that you are likely receiving more energy and information than your system can manage and it could end up with a sensory overload. Calming yourself is the most important thing you can do. You can meditate and take a rest when this happens.

- Overthinking is also one of the causes of excess energy because our thoughts are incredibly powerful. Our thoughts draw to us the very thing that we are thinking about, both on spiritual and physical levels. If you are stuck in a thought, you are likely to be overwhelmed with emotions, and without a balance of taking appropriate actions to deal with it, then the energy is building up without a place to go. You can connect with your spirit guide and ask them to help you and guide you in which way you should go so that you can process and use your energy in a healthier way.

- Unresolved emotions also cause excess emotions. When life events happen to us that we cannot control and we are left with a life lesson and lots of emotions, it is important to process your feelings and integrate the lessons that you are meant to learn. If you do not process these feelings, you will end up locking this energy into your mind and the world will bring you more events that will trigger that lesson and feelings until you are ready to do the internal work that you are supposed to do and learn the lesson that you need to learn. Having a full range of emotions is healthy and embracing and feeling your emotions with compassion is extremely important. Our world is a mirror to psychic empaths, just consider that if you are willing to look at your emotions honestly and with compassion, you will also attract other people that also do the same. To process your unresolved emotions and clear the energies in your body, you can try writing them in a journal and exercise a release of energy. You can also take a clearing bath to help this process.

- Toxic people and environments are a big source of negative energies and most of them will turn into excess energy if you do not process them. When people do not process or express their emotions in a healthy way, it accumulates and can stick to you and your environment. Every one of us does it, but some people do it as a way of life. In our case, we have the choice to process our emotions and learn to return ourselves to love and peace but for others, it is all about creating boundaries to avoid the negativity that they bring. Spending too much time around these people or spaces will eventually start to affect your energy. Proper energy hygiene is critical and understanding that these people and environment are also a part of our life, so instead of resenting them, you should embrace it and also do your part. The most powerful thing you can do is honor and process how these people make you feel then change that into a positive perspective. It may be a situation that is happening, again and again, then that means that you already know what to expect and that means that you know how to prepare for engaging with this type of people and places.

- Cluttered places and hoarding unnecessary items also cause excess energy for us psychic empaths. Your space is a reflection of yourself and your energy. If you have a cluttered place, you will not be able to find the things that you need and if you hold into every memento that passes through your hands then it is a clear sign that you are also holding onto a lot of mental energies, emotional energies, and memories as well. Hoarding can be extreme or as simple as being overly sentimental and attaching too much emotion to objects and things. The inability to let these things go in our environment is a sign of not being able to let go of a lot of your emotions and thoughts. Ask yourself what are you afraid of letting go, and why are you afraid of it. The answer may surprise you. You can donate things you have not used in the past year to let the energy go and make sure to do a clearing bath afterward. Meditation also helps to clear your mind after letting go of the things that you valued for a long time. It may be hard but you can start small and move on to getting rid of more kinds of stuff along the way.

CHAPTER 3: HOW TO KNOW IF YOU ARE A PSYCHIC EMPATH

Signs Saying That You Are A Psychic Empath

Psychic empaths are able to intensely feel the emotions of other beings, such as animals, plants, and other people. Sometimes they can feel the emotions of others even more than their own feelings and emotions. Do you feel like you are often deeply in tune with the feelings of other people around you? Would you or someone close to you call yourself a very sensitive person? Does being in a place with lots of people make you uncomfortable? If your answer to all those questions is yes, then you might be a psychic empath. Here are the signs that say if you are a psychic empath:

Almost Never Get Sick

If you are a psychic empath, chances are you almost never get sick because of the enhanced healing energy that is inside you. One of the abilities of a psychic empath is to be able to heal themselves and other people by sensing the healing energies inside a person and amplifying it. And you are able to heal your sickness before they even manifest without you even knowing that you are doing it. As long as you are not overwhelmed with negative energies, you will be able to heal yourself and not get sick most of the time.

You Feel Connected To Animals And Nature

More often than not, most people really find comfort, serenity, and peace in nature. However, psychic empaths are more drawn towards not only nature itself but also nature in remote areas where they can enjoy themselves in the solitude of their being. They are also more connected to animals because they can also sense and feel the emotions of an animal. Some psychic empaths are also able to communicate with an animal and can tell what an animal wants. They are also able to make the animal understand what they are trying to say to that animal.

You Avoid Crowds

Another indication that tells that you might be a psychic empath is that you tend to drown out in the crowd so you try to avoid it as much as possible. This is because being in a crowd will make you easily absorb all the positive and negative energies and emotions of the other people that are in the crowd. You might find it overwhelming and hard to handle the emotional noise that is coming from the crowd, especially if you are there for an extended period of time. This may cause you to feel physically unwell.

You Tend To Stay Alone

Since you find it hard to be exposed in a crowd, you will most likely just want to be alone instead. You find comfort in shutting out the world because you find peace and healing by doing so. When your favorite activities include taking your time alone outdoors or meditating alone in a quiet place, then you might be a psychic empath.

You Have An Odd Ability To Perceive Patterns

Psychic empaths have an odd ability to perceive patterns because of their highly sensitive intuition. They are able to predict certain things because they see a pattern that is in that certain scenario. This is also connected to their ability to sense and feel other people's feelings and emotions. Once they sense other people's energy, they are able to associate it with certain things like a flower for example. And they will find a pattern to see why that certain person is feeling the way he is feeling. If you are able to see a lot of patterns in your day-to-day life or in other people, then you might be a psychic empath.

People Flock To You For Help

Because of the abundance of positive energy that is coming from a psychic empath. Other people will be unconsciously drawn to you. This is because they can feel that you will be able to help them with their problems and they know that it will be hard for you to say no to them because of the love and kindness in your heart.

Your Dreams Come True

If you are having dreams that are coming true. It might be a vision sent to you in your sleep by your spirit guide. These dreams are often there to help guide you in what you should do in the upcoming situation or it can be a warning for you to be prepared for something that is about to happen. If you feel like your dreams are coming true or you feel like you have been in a certain situation that you think that already happened, then you might be a psychic empath.

Electromagnetic Hypersensitivity

Electromagnetic hypersensitivity means that you are extra sensitive to the electromagnetic fields that are coming from electronic devices such as computers and smartphones. Symptoms of electromagnetic hypersensitivity can include having headaches, mood issues, dizziness, memory difficulties, having a hard time getting sleep, and having trouble concentrating. Psychic empaths have electromagnetic hypersensitivity because the electromagnetic fields that come from the electronic device are similar to the energies that are coming from other people, animals, and nature but it is not meant to be sent to us psychic empaths. That is why we may feel sick if we are exposed to electronic fields.

You Attract People Who Needed To Be Saved

Psychic empath's abilities can help many people in many ways. You can help them identify and deal with the emotions that they are having. A psychic empath can also heal not only their physical illness but also the illness in their hearts. You can mend relationships and turn negative energies into positive energics. That is why people who need to be saved are attracted to you. But be careful because you also need to take care of yourself and not just other people. Do not overwork yourself and give yourself time to rest and recover all the energies that you spend while helping other people.

Aura Reading

An aura reading is a process in which a psychic empath begins to tap into another person's energy field to reveal the other person's personality, motives, and purpose. The aura colors are a tool given to us by the universe to help us recognize a person's overall personality. Seeing what the issues are in a person's energy will allow them to be more responsible with their energy, to help them make better and more genuine choices in their lives, and move past walls and other hurdles in their life that they have been conditioned to live with.

What Is An Aura

The main purpose of aura reading is to embrace yourself for who you really are. Auras are described as an electromagnetic field that surrounds a person's body and is associated with energy signature around every person. Understanding your aura can help you live your life more truthfully in every aspect of your life such as your career, money, motivation, and relationship with yourself and other people. Auras can also be contagious, which is why you may start to feel extra happy if you are around someone with a positive aura and you might feel drained when you are around someone with a negative aura. Aura is like a personality type and it has a certain color that represents each personality type.

Aura Colors And Their Meaning

While there are different layers and colors to each person's aura that all mean different things, every person has one predominant aura color that represents their personality. Also, take note that a person's aura can change depending on their current state of mind but it will most likely return to its original color once everything is settled down. Like when you are experiencing an extreme mood change due to a horrible friend, your aura will most likely reflect that. Other things like physical and emotional trauma or illness can also affect your aura color.

1. White – A white aura shows a well-balanced person-ality, one that is calm and open to all possibilities. This color of the aura is the rarest of all aura colors.

2. Black – A black aura can represent dark energy which is often pessimistic and unkind. A person with this color of the aura is most likely filled with lots of neg-ative energy.

3. Grey – A grey aura can show uncertainty and skepti-cism about other people and situations. A person with this aura color can be filled with doubts and would most likely not try something new.

4. Brown – A brown aura or tan aura color often repre-sents career-drive and a person who loves working with their hand. People with this aura color are very logical and practical, they are the type of friend that has a strict budget and a detailed long-term plan. They know that hard work and strategy can get them to where they want to go.

5. Red – A red aura means that a person is confident, aggressive, and strong. They are passionate, goal-ori-ented, and love to take charge. They are ambitious, brave, and never back down from a challenge.

6. Pink – A pink aura indicates that a person has a ro-mantic and gentle soul. Unlike people with red auras,

people with pink aura like peace and harmony more than anything. They usually end a fight before it can even begin. Everyone around them loves their kind and calming energy.

7. Magenta – A magenta aura means that a person is very independent. They are creative and funny, the ones who many people like to watch. They make trends instead of following one. Some people might think that magenta aura people are weird but deep down, they only admire the individuality of the person with a magenta aura.

8. Orange – An orange aura represents being energetic and lively. People with this aura color are most likely in good health and have a lot of energy to do things. They are the type of people that always try to work out in a gym. They are optimistic and sociable, and they make friends easily. They get along with almost everyone because of their positivity and they are usually always in a good mood.

9. Yellow – A yellow aura represents optimism, intelligence, and freedom. People with this aura color are always very full of life. Communication is their strong point, they might be a talkative person or a prolific writer. They love to have fun and tend to take life less seriously. They are witty, smart, and confident. That is why other people want to be like them.

10. Green – A green aura represents growth and healing. People with this aura love nature. They develop self-

love, overcome problems, and forgive those who wronged them. They are compassionate and open. They tend to have a practical worldview. They are likely to be influenced by their surroundings, which is why it is important for them to make time and go out in nature, whether it be just simply turning off their phone, going camping for a week, or just taking a walk in a park.

11. Blue – A person with a blue aura is caring, empathetic, and sensitive. They take life more seriously than other aura colors. They are expressive and creative, and they place a lot of value on close personal relationships like their family members and their closest friends. They value truth and honesty, so they do not like people who lie to them.

12. Indigo – The indigo aura indicates that a person is both very creative and very shy. They are often off at a corner in a party, silently thinking about creative things such as composing a song or writing a book. They have strong intuition and they are curious people. They always want to learn more and find out what the truth is.

13. Violet – A violet aura indicates that a person is wise, spiritual, and artistic. They often daydream or get lost in their fantasy. They are very intuitive, very spiritual, and have a strong gut feeling. The people that surround them value their empathy and wisdom, even if other people do not always understand them.

How To Read A Person's Aura

It is possible to learn to see your own aura, you may see it in a mirror by clearing your mind and focusing on trying to sense your aura. It is helpful to do this while you are meditating and you are visualizing your aura. You can also connect with your spirit guide and ask them to show you your aura. Sometimes, you might not be able to see your aura right away but you will definitely feel that it is there. After a few practices and once you are starting to get comfortable with reading your own aura, you can try to move on to reading your friend's or family's aura.

Benefits Of Aura Reading

An aura reading can help you or other people keep your own feelings and emotions in check. You may be giving off negative energy even if you are not aware of it or you could be allowing other people's energies to affect you more than you even realize. Knowing and understanding your aura can also help you understand yourself and know what it is that you truly desire. It can also help you identify other people's intentions if they are good or not and you can avoid them or help guide them into a better path.

Intuition

Intuition is a form of knowledge that comes from our consciousness without obvious deliberation. It is a feeling in which hunches are made by our unconscious mind with the help of the universe. Sometimes referred to as gut feelings, because we feel it near our stomach, more specifically in our solar plexus which is the center of our feelings and emotions, intuition tends to arise quickly and without awareness of the underlying processing of information.

In simple words, intuition is the feeling that we have that guides us on what to do. Like sensing when to make a career change or you have a feeling about a certain situation or person, for example, when you knew something was wrong with your friend or that you could not trust a particular person because something about him does not feel right.

Vivid Dreams

When we sleep, we do not just recharge our body, our mind is very busy during our sleep. We dream all of the time, we sometimes just wake up and have no idea what we have dreamed about because we forget about it as soon as we wake up. However, psychic empaths can closely recall all of their dreams because their dreams are intense. These are called vivid dreams. Dreams that we do not just forget easily. Dreams can sometimes be soothing or scary, mysterious or helpful, and realistic or fantastical.

Psychic empaths regularly have vivid dreams that they remember, it is an experience that starts in their childhood. This is because they are attracted to the dream world and they look forward to sleeping each night. Dreams are such a powerful form of intuition because they bypass the ego and the linear mind to deliver clear intuitive information. They bring guidance about healing, spirituality, and overcoming difficult emotions, teaching you how to help yourself and how you can help others.

Your spirit guide may also communicate with you during your sleep. They may appear in many forms such as spirit animals, deceased loved ones, or angels. They may tell you how to overcome obstacles, reach your goals, or lead you to a more spiritual and peaceful life. Spirit guides provide helpful, compassionate information, and never anything that is harmful to you or to other people around you.

Psychic empaths can also travel to other realms while they are dreaming. They might even feel more comfortable in their dreams than they do when they are awake. To develop your dream-related abilities, keep a dream journal and write down all the details of your dream that you can remember every morning. Upon waking up, spend a few quiet moments in the hypnagogic state, the state where you are in the middle of sleeping and waking up, and record whatever parts of your dreams that you can remember. Then you can think about the meaning of the information from your dream throughout your day.

You should also get in the habit of asking a question before you go to sleep. Questions that ask about what directions shall you take your career or if the relationship you have with a certain person is good for the both of you. Then in the next morning, see how the answer in your dream applies to the question that you asked from the night before. Regularly remembering and learning from your dreams will be beneficial and can help you more deeply understand your-self and other people around you.

Release Resistance

Resistance is a term that refers to the impartial force or collection of negative energy that you hold within you which prevents you from obtaining your goal. It can be any thought, belief, or behavior, that may either be conscious or unconscious, that stands in our way of getting what we want. One example is when you believe that you are vulnerable or susceptible to something that you do not want and you are holding yourself back because you are afraid to do something wrong and fail. But this only prevents you from getting your goal and it holds you in a place where you are not letting in the positivity that you would receive otherwise. Our mind is a very powerful tool. If you do not believe that you can get something that you want, it shows up as resistance and despite all the things that you are doing to achieve your goal, you will still be held back by that resistance. Here are a few helpful tips to help you release resistance from your consciousness:

1. **Be Honest With Yourself and Acknowledge Your Resistance**

   The first step to releasing your resistance is being honest with yourself and acknowledging your resistance. We have to understand that even though our loving mindset wants to be at peace, our fearful ego does not want us to give up judgment, to be free, or to release control because it is afraid and filled with doubts. When we accept and acknowledge that we are afraid and have resistance, we will be able to forgive ourselves for being afraid and we can look for a better way to handle ourselves. You should be honest and clear on how you want to deal with your resistance, ask yourself what is holding you back from doing what you want, and forgive it. Resistance will continue to show up in our lives and that is okay, acknowledge it and forgive yourself so that you can return to your path as soon as possible.

2. Do Not Judge Everything And Accept Them

When we judge an external circumstance, whether reflected through other people's actions, our life circumstances, or our own judgments, we will start to think that those circumstances are not ok. This will imply that something in your environment needs to change in order for you to be better. Judgment implies that you are not able to be, do, or have anything that you want.

Acceptance, on the other hand, allows your current situation to pass through you more easily. When you accept something for what it is when it is in front of you at that moment, you allow the thought to pass through you. Work on improving your level of ease and acceptance to all areas of your life to be able to release resistance.

In most cases, judgment has been our greatest defense mechanism. We judge things to defend against our vulnerability. We are afraid that if we let our guard down and act kind and lovingly towards someone, we might get taken advantage of and will no longer be safe. The more aware we become of how we use judgment to play it safe, then the more we can realize how unsafe things really are. We will begin to see that judgment only leads to more judgment. When you try to protect yourself by judging others, you create more separation and you will deepen your disconnection from love. Love can seem scarier to us than fear. We are terrified to let love into our life because we are afraid that when we do, we will only be exposed to more pain. But that is not the case, love is the antidote to judgment and it will heal everything and get rid of all the pain.

3. Do Something About The Things You Can Act-On

If you ever encounter something that you have no control over, you should let go of it and focus more on the things that you can act on. Sometimes, becoming aware of your repetitive patterns is all that you need. But other times, we need to take additional actions. If you are in a place of resistance about something, look for the fear that is causing the resistance and find a way to dissipate it. Meditation is one example of a way to help you dissipate fear, but you can also arm yourself with knowledge. Knowing more about the things that we are afraid of can help us understand them better and we will not be as scared of it because fear often comes from the unknown. You can also tell yourself something else to take your focus off away from the thing that you are afraid of. Talking to a friend or a family member can also help. But the most important thing is to take action, if you can do something about it, do it.

4. Focus On Something Else

When you think about the thing that you want and why you want it so much, resistance in the form of frustrations, thoughts, feelings, or conscious and unconscious beliefs, is usually also present at the same time. If you distract yourself entirely by thinking about something else that you like, you will be in a much calmer and more relaxed phase of allowing. And the universe will bring you the thing that you want with the least amount of resistance. This is why people who fall in love usually drop the extra weight that they have been carrying for a long time or get a promotion that they have been wanting before. They are in a state where they are open to receiving the gifts of the universe for them. Remember that things are delivered to us on our path and sometimes it requires less effort than we think. But we should go out of our way and feel worthy of receiving them. That is what we have to do.

5. Try To Find Something That Will Make You Change Perspective

Try to find something that will make you change your perspective in life and repeat them as often as you can. Look for inspiration and make it your new mantra. Instead of saying that it always never happens for you, think that it can happen to you and it will happen to you, eventually, you will get what you want if you attract it. Ask the universe to give you proof that what you want is possible and then take notice of what kind of sign will come to you. Pay attention to everything you see like billboards, books that people hand to you, articles that you happen to stumble upon, or the people that you meet. We often look at where other people are and compare ourselves to them but we forget to pay attention to who they were before they got to the place where they are now. There are plenty of rags to riches stories out there. Look for the story that resonates the most with where you are and let that be your new possibility. If it can happen to them, then it can happen to you as well.

6. Ask Your Spirit Guide For Help

We have always been taught to be afraid of everything that we do not know in the world. One of the most common ways we believe in the fear of the world is by doubting ourselves and, as a result, we are resisting love by trying to control our lives in the wrong way by holding ourselves back. Releasing your resistances requires mental reprogramming. You should surrender yourself and stop trying to control everything. Ask your spirit guide for support and guidance to help yourself be able to be at peace and release your resistance. You can ask your spirit guide while you are meditating. Tell them that you surrender all your goals and plans to their care. Open up yourself and accept the spiritual guidance that they will give you. Trust that there is a plan far greater than yours. Know that when you are feeling that you are not enough and you feel like you have plenty of limitations, spiritual solutions will help you and give you creative ideas. Step back and let love lead your way and everything else that you want will follow.

7. Focus Your Attention More On The Present

Another powerful tool for releasing resistance is to focus your attention more on the present moment. Most of our negative energies come from a situation that is not actually happening right now. We carry over past events, often feeling guilty, ashamed, or having regret, and we try to anticipate and worry about the future too much. If you can learn to relax your mind and turn away from these tendencies, and bring a clearer appreciation of everything that is happening in the present, then you will see that most of your internal resistance will disappear.

Not only will you release this unnecessary negativity, but focusing on the present can also help you see the incredible power of being present in the moment. This means that you will be more aware of your situation and it will help you develop yourself to be better and you will experience better feelings of joy and happiness. Becoming more mindful will also increase your physical sense perceptions, so you begin to find more richness in your life.

8. Increase Your Trust In Yourself And In The Positive Outcome

Releasing your resistance is linked to our ability to develop a strong sense of trust. If you trust and believe in yourself more, the less likely it is that you will worry about the small things that do not go your way. If you trust in yourself and you believe that everything will work out for you, you will not have to worry about what each little thing and action means, and you can instead relax and enjoy your life more and focus on the more important things in your life.

9. Always Choose To Be Happy

We have an important responsibility to make ourselves happy most of the time. The happier we are, the more positivity will come to us and everything around us. We will have more power to express our presence and have more positive energy we can put out to the world. When we lean towards happiness, we raise our vibrational frequency which gives us the energy that we need to show up and do the things that we are meant to do. Joy is the inspiration behind creative ideas and solutions for seemingly hopeless problems. It provides us with the generosity that is required so that we can give more to someone that is in need. And when you are happy, you will also make everyone around you also happy and you will spread more positive energy to yourself and the world around you.

Connect To Mother Earth

Some empaths are keenly attuned to our natural world and all of the Earth's movements. The beauty of a waterfall, the tranquility of a forest, and the calmness of a night shore can energize them, while toxicity from different kinds of pollution can make them feel sick, extremely tired, or very sad. They can sensually and energetically feel the strength of a thunderstorm, the loveliness of the moon, and the warmth of the sun on their skin. What happens to the Earth is closely connected to the well-being of their body and mind. Their energy is nourished and sustained from the energy of the Earth and our universe. The Earth and the universe love a psychic empath and they can feel it. They experience the changes in the Earth as if it were things that were happening to them so when the Earth is in a positive state then they also feel happy. Psychic empaths can have visions about an upcoming natural disaster or they can feel them intensely in their body while it is currently happening. If you think that you are a psychic empath, you should be aware of how your body will react during a dramatic change in the Earth so that you can put your feelings and emotions into consideration and practice taking care of yourself when they happen.

You may also be sensitive to solar flares. Solar flares are magnetic storms that are happening on the sun that affect the magnetic fields around the Earth and your body. Natural disasters such as hurricanes, tornados, earthquakes, and sometimes even volcanic eruptions will most likely happen after strong solar activity. During these times, you may experience some negative effects happening to you such as headaches, anxiety, mood swings, or even heart palpitations. Always remember that the sun is the one that is responsible for giving life to the Earth and when it goes through changes, we will be able to feel it even if it is millions of miles away from us.

To stay energized and positive, one of the ways you can take care of yourself is by connecting with the Earth more frequently. Here are some simple ways you can connect with the Earth:

1. **Spend More Time With Nature**

   Spend more time in the mountains, in forests, or by the beach where you can interact and connect with nature and you will feel more at home and in peace. Go for a walk, watch the sunset, look at the stars at night, swim in lakes, rivers, or sea, hug a tree, and try to take some of the things that you do outdoors instead of staying indoors such as yoga practice, meditation, or even eating lunch with a friend.

2. Eat Clean, Healthy, and Organic Foods

You should also eat clean, healthy, and organic foods to help you deepen your connection with the Earth. Eating junk foods and other processed food will make you less connected with the world because you are not consuming the Earth's energies.

3. Feel The Earth Beneath Your Feet

Take your shoes off and stand on a grassy field, try to feel the sensations that the Earth gives you. Close your eyes and take a couple of deep breaths while you focus on the connection that you have with the Earth. You can also lie flat on your back and try to soak up the Earth's positive energies.

4. Grow Something

Whether it is a small flower in a pot, a vegetable patch, a few seeds by your window sill, or a small garden outside your house, taking care of a plant is one of the best ways to be connected with nature. They give off a positive energy that can help you feel good and energized.

Listen To Yourself

Listening to yourself is an important thing to do for a psychic empath because sometimes we may get lost in the sea of emotions that we sense from all the other people that are around us. Listening to yourself will help you understand yourself more and take care of yourself to reach the goal that you have. You may spend your whole life thinking that you are on track and it may seem like you are on a path of success but you will wake up one day and realize that you are not actually happy. This is because there is a good chance that you have never stopped and listened to yourself to understand what it is that you actually want and will truly make you happy. Here are the steps to help you learn to listen to yourself and cultivate your relationship with yourself:

1. **Learn About What Values You Have**

    The values that you have are what truly matter to you. If you do not know what your true values are, and you are living out ones that are not really fit for you then you might always feel restless and not content. To find out what your values are, take a look at your life and which of your choices bring you joy and excitement without a doubt. If you think that your value is money but you feel like you hate your job as a financial advisor and you love volunteering more, then it is possible that your true value is giving. If you are not sure if a value you think is yours is really yours, then you should try imagining your life where you spend it living only that specific value. If you think your value is power, you should imagine a life where all you have to do is give out commands and instructions by yourself every single day. Will that make you happy or would you feel lonely? If you do not think that it will give you happiness then maybe your true value is actually leadership. Think of where your value comes from and evaluate if it is truly yours or it is just something you cling to because someone close to you such as a friend or family member also has that value.

2. Think About Your Core Beliefs And Reevaluate Them

The core beliefs that you have are viewpoints about others, your life, and yourself that you have taken to be fact. But in reality, they are simply just beliefs that you have chosen to take in your life. Oftentimes these beliefs came from your childhood and are passed down to you by your parents and family. They are the things that say something like the world is filled with danger in every corner, trust only yourself because you cannot trust anyone, or that money is the cause of all the selfishness and wicked actions in the world. The problem with such core beliefs is that you may not recognize them and they will run your unconscious mind and affect all your decisions until you make them stop. They can also hinder you from listening to yourself, especially if those beliefs are in contrast with who you have become now. It requires hard work to understand and be honest about what your core beliefs are and to try to find out what they really are, and sometimes it may require assistance from a counselor or you may need to contact your spirit guide for help. But removing the ones that cause you to make bad decisions and replacing them with ones that bring more positivity to your life is a truly helpful process.

3. Try To Learn More About Your Inner Critic

Your inner critic is the voice inside your head that criticizes, judges, or sometimes demeans you whether the self-criticism is objectively justified or not. An inner critic that is always active can take a toll on a psychic empath's emotional well-being and confidence. A lot of people may have a hard time dealing with their self-esteem and confidence, even when they seem like they are confident, successful, or well-adjusted to the world. A person's inner critic can be a nonstop nagging voice that questions each of your decisions and undermines every one of your accomplishments. This can cause a person to have difficult feelings such as shame, inadequacy, guilt or self-doubt. People usually develop an inner critic as a result of a negative life experience.

Pay attention to each of your thoughts every day and try to recognize if it is your inner critic talking. Do not take what your inner critic says to you personally because most of the time it is untrue and you are an amazing and wonderful human being that deserves love and positivity in your life.

4. Clear Your Mind

One of the reasons why you might be struggling to listen to your true self is because you just have so many thoughts and it is like you are trying to find one paperclip in a desk that has so much clutter. Aside from the inner critic that we already talked about previously, you might also be listening to your inner child that is causing you to wallow in self-pity by saying things like nothing that you do matters or nobody loves you and cares for you. And that might make you suffer from anxiety attacks and make you worry more about the past and the future events in your life.

So, how can we really hear our true self through all the chatter in our mind? A good practice to try is to get a pen and a notebook to try to do a thing called free form journaling. Just write down as fast as you can everything that is going on in your head, all the judgements, the sadness, the anger, and the self-criticism that comes to your mind. Do not worry if what you are writing is legible or not.

What will happen is that you will find yourself writing your way through all your mind clutters to your true voice. At the beginning, it may take you some time to write a single sentence or two that feels like your true self saying what it truly wants, but if you practice this exercise often, you might find your real voice showing up not long after the pen hits the first page. Some people can even try to do this technique of clearing their mind by speaking out loud instead of writing it down. Rant out all the things that are annoying you or are worrying you until you hear yourself saying something that resonates within you. Just remember to be careful and do it in a private place where you are sure no one can hear you.

5. Be Mindful

One more extremely effective way of clearing your mind clutter and to listen to your true self is mindfulness. Mindfulness is paying attention and being aware of the present moment on purpose and not judging. Meditation can help you feel more conscious and more aware for the rest of your day. Focusing on only one thing at a time can also help you be mindful. If you practice being mindful every day, you will find yourself becoming more and more efficient at being able to zone in and identify how you really are feeling at the current moment.

6. Pay Attention To Your Imagination

Your rational mind and logical mind are just parts of yourself and if you are only listening to them then you are not truly listening to yourself. If you are listening to yourself and you think about something that sounds outrageous but you truly want it, instead of stopping yourself and thinking that it is impossible, try imagining what could happen and see what comes to you and try to use your creativity and imagine a "what if" scenario.

7. Always Ask Yourself Good Questions

A question that starts with either "what" or "how" are oftentimes a good question, while questions that start with "why" will often lead you down a confusing or nonsensical situation that is difficult to escape or to self-criticism. On the other hand, "what" and "how" questions are questions that lead you to look forward and come up with solutions to a problem.

Try asking yourself extraordinary and wild questions about your future to learn more things about yourself that might surprise even you. For example, if you were given a lot of money to spend however you want, what will you spend your money on? If you were spending time with whoever you want to do anything you would want to do, what would you do? If you have a month left to live, how would you spend your last remaining time here on earth?

8. **Try Out New Things Regularly**

A lot of us think that we surely know what we really like but in reality, we are just doing the things that we have been taught are the right things to do, things that someone close to us did or is currently doing. Try to avoid being sucked into this kind of false mindset by trying out things that you have never tried before, at least once a week or as often as you can. Try taking a different exercise class at the gym, try new foreign foods that you have never eaten before, or try talking to someone that you would not think you have anything in common with. Some of the things you try might be a failure and you might end up not liking them but every now and then, you will come across something that did not know you like because you have not tried it before and that may lead you to a path of discovering a new part of yourself that you have not discovered before.

9. **Learn To Let Go**

Holding on to the things that are already not fit for you is like building a wall that is holding you back and preventing you from accessing your true self. This also includes relationships. If you are always spending time and hanging around with people who you no longer have anything in common with and deep down you are not sure if you even like them anymore, just because you have known them for a very long time, then you are stopping yourself from reaching your true potential and you are not being true to yourself.

10. Spend More Time To Take Care Of Yourself

Just like how you trust your friend that is the kindest to you the most, you may also find that you might open up to yourself more if you are nicer to yourself and you practice self-care. Self-care will often create time for you to hear yourself because you will be calmer and more relaxed. Think about how you can treat yourself nicely, is it by taking a long warm bath instead of engaging in a social activity that you do not really want to go to? Or is it finally working on properly managing your finances so that you can stop worrying?

If lately you are experiencing a lot of anxiety and you find it really hard to listen to yourself or find out who you really are, you might want to go to a counsellor or therapist as it is also a form of self-care. They are trained at not only listening to you but also at asking you just the right questions to help you discover parts of yourself that you have not known yet about before.

So, coming to them might lead you to hearing yourself in a way that you were not aware was possible.

Not listening to yourself can lead to a psychological struggle, as well as the tendency to fulfill someone else's idea of happiness and success instead of your own. This may include being codependent, where you take your identity from pleasing other people instead of taking it from who you really are. It can also involve depression because it feels draining and very tiring to feel lost inside your own self. If you are having a hard time struggling to know who you really are at all, you feel like you change completely or lose yourself in every relationship you are in, and you cannot stop making impulsive decisions, there is a chance that you may have a borderline personality disorder, which requires additional support from professionals. It takes commitment and effort to know the difference between the things you have been taught to believe that is true versus what is really true for your own self. But your effort will be worth it because when you truly know how to listen to yourself carefully, you are going to make choices that lead towards the life that you truly want and not the one you think you should want. And that will lower your stress levels for sure and raise your confidence and being content.

Mystic Capabilities

Having a strong intuitive ability gives a psychic empath mystic capability. A psychic empath can gather information from the universe using their strong hyper sensory perception. A psychic empath is making use of the four main avenues that our intuition uses to communicate with us, also known as the "Four Clairs" in the psychic circles, clairvoyance or the ability to see images, clairaudience or the ability to hear voices, clairsentience or the ability to recognize feelings, and claircognizance or the ability to know something. While some psychics can be naturally more adept in utilizing one of the four clairs, all of us can improve our intuition by practicing it and trying out new methods.

The Four "Clairs" Of The Psychic Circle

1. **Clairvoyance Or The Ability To See Images**

   Most people who are not well versed with psychic terminologies usually use the term clairvoyant as if it has the same meaning as psychic, but in reality, clairvoyance is just one of the abilities that a psychic empath has. Clairvoyant transmissions, which is sent to a psychic in the form of an image or scenery in his mind, is usually coming in as a metaphor and not literal. If someone is overwhelmed or struggling, you might see them in your vision that they are drowning or carrying a large boulder on their shoulders. If you see an image of the earth shifting its continental plates or the ground is moving under someone's feet, it may mean that the client is currently experiencing a very big change in their life and that they feel like nothing is stable. If you see them fishing and there are a lot of small fishes swimming by their fishing line, it might mean that the client is looking for a new job or a business opportunity and they should wait for a big fish or a really good offer that will be beneficial to them. These are just a few examples of what you may see when you look at a person, the images are usually different for each person so try to think about what your vision can mean.

To develop your clairvoyance abilities, you should pay attention to all the images that may pop up into your mind out of the blue because they may be intuitive messages. These images may also come in your dreams so pay attention to that too. Just be patient because it may take a long time to develop your clairvoyance depending if you are more inclined to it or not.

2. Clairaudience Or The Ability To Hear Voices

Clairaudient messages are sounds you hear that seem like someone is talking to you in your mind. This voice will never be harsh on you or cause you discomfort unlike the other voices that people usually hear when they have a severe hormonal imbalance, psychological condition, or vitamin and mineral deficiencies. The tone of the voice that sends you a clairaudient message is always calm, relaxed, and clear. Clairaudient messages that may arrive to you during your meditations or if you are doing a psychic reading on someone are usually something that is very straightforward and literal. For example, you may hear something like "wait for the right time" or "find a new job". Clairaudient messages are often short messages and sometimes the message will only be one word or number. For example, you may receive the message that someone's subconscious roadblocks are triggered by an event that is very traumatic for them when she was at the age of "twelve" or that someone might want to change their current career and their next career should be "teaching" or that someone's partner is named "Earl". And while you may hear something cliché most of the time like "this is the right time", "he is the one", or "she only wants something that she cannot have", clairaudient messages can sometimes also be poetic.

To develop your clairaudient abilities, you may try to spend more time with other psychic empaths that specialize in their clairaudient abilities. Some people say that they clearly heard someone calling their name but it turns out that there is no one there after they turned around and looked after they had a psychic reading with a clairaudient psychic empath. You can also try to listen to the things in your mind while you are meditating.

3. Clairsentience Or The Ability To Recognize Feelings

Clairsentient messages are messages that you receive as a feeling, and this is the most common ability among the four clairs. Being able to read the emotions, feelings of other people or sensing the collective energy of a room and your gut feeling all fall under this category. Before you talk to someone, you can usually get a feeling for their energy and personality. They may be serious, bubbly, outgoing, shy, highly intellectual, or nurturing. Whenever you tell someone a message and you get a feeling of chills all over your body, this indicates that the message you gave to that person is something very important for them to hear. If someone near you has a physical ailment, you may often feel them briefly in your body during or before you talk to them. Your shoulders may feel a pain if the person had a surgery in that area or a sensation may run through your stomach if the person has a digestive issue. Your throat may also feel tight if the person's throat chakra is closed off or in other words, their expression of themselves and their emotions is closed off to other people.

To develop your clairsentience ability, you should write down in a journal whenever you get a strong intuitive feeling about something or someone. Over the course of the next couple of weeks or months, you may begin to realize how many clairsentient messages you are getting from your intuition. And once you begin to realize that these messages are clairsentient messages, then it will help you be able to pick them up more often.

4. Claircognizance Or The Ability To Know Something

Knowing that a certain someone's parents have a narcissistic personality or if someone's child is very sensitive even though you have not met the child is the intuitive ability called claircognizance. It is the ability to know something without being informed about it. It is when your brain gets immediate information from our intuition, just like when you download a huge amount of data from the internet into the hard drive of your computer. Although the download that happens to a human brain only occurs within a few seconds. You do not need to wait for a long time for a large file to load because our connection to our intuition is fast and efficient. You also can be able to tell if someone has an old emotional wound that is holding them back or you can instantly understand a complex relationship with two persons that are friends or colleagues because of claircognizance.

To develop your claircognizance ability, you can silently ask your intuition to give you answers when your logical brain is stumped and it cannot provide you with an answer when you are trying to figure something out. Whether it is your friend's motivation to do something or the quickest way to finish your morning errands. Our intuition is always listening to us and could give us amazing answers that we would not be able to think about if we only use our logical brain to think.

Intuition Pitfalls

If you are new to listening to your intuitions and you respond to certain things without always thinking things out thoroughly first or you are reasoning why you feel the way you do. You are relying only on your experience to guide you in the correct path, this is where your intuition can lead you off course to where you should be going. You may not understand how much experience you actually have in yourself and regardless, your reaction to different situations will be different for each of the circumstances that you experience. To be able to make your intuition more useful and reliable, you should learn more about it and hone your intuitive skills. There are four stages of our intuitive competence:

- Stage 1 – Unconscious Competence, this is the stage where our intuition is wrong and we are producing poor quality outcomes when we listen to it without us even realizing it.

- Stage 2 – Conscious Competence, this is the stage where we are using our logical brain to think and do the analysis of a situation but our analysis is wrong and we are aware that the outcome is of poor quality because of this.

- Stage 3 – Unconscious Competence, this is the stage where the logical analysis of our mind is correct and we can produce good quality results when we are following the defined steps that we think about.

- Stage 4 – Conscious Competence, this is the stage where our intuition is correct and we intuitively produce good quality outcomes by relying on our intuitions.

At any given point of our life, we might be at one or more of these stages. Maybe you are very good at designing something and your creativity is at a high point, it means that you are at stage 4. If you are new at something that you have not tried before then you may be at stage 1. Or If you are able to follow the process of designing something but you are not sure what the overall aesthetic should be, then you are at both stage 3 and stage 2, stage 3 at the design process and stage 2 at the overall aesthetic. And since two out of four stages are unconscious stages, it may be difficult for you to confidently judge the solutions you are trying to choose from. Which is why it is important to know your competence so that you are able to deal with your intuitions accordingly.

Three Obstacles That Prevent Us From Following Our Intuitions

Aside from knowing your competence level, there are also three obstacles that are in your way of following your intuitions, these are fear, lack of confidence, and lack of trust.

1. **Fear**

    When we are faced with a major dilemma and either choice will have a consequence but one choice just feels more right than the other choice, that is our intuition telling us that we know the right decision and we should listen to our intuition. But we may also be afraid and hear another voice in the back of our mind telling us that what if we are wrong and we just end up looking like a fool, we would not want to look like a fool right so it is telling us to just ignore our intuition instead. This is when we enter into a state of self-doubt and negative thinking. The fear of making the wrong decision or hurting someone by choosing a certain decision is what is getting in our way of listening to our own intuition. Fear stops us from acting on our intuition and listening to it. And most of the time, that voice that is stopping us from listening to our intuition is usually the wrong one and our intuition is correct all along. To overcome our fear of listening to our own intuition, we should remind ourselves that, even though we may not have said anything in the past, our intuition is always right. Think about what will happen if you do not listen to your intuition, is it worth giving away the positive outcome that your intuition is leading you to and giving into the fear when you might be able to avoid a lot of problems in the future instead?

2. Lack Of Confidence

Maybe you are new to your job or business and you do not feel totally comfortable in your current situation yet, and you are lacking the confidence that you once had in the past when you are in a situation where you are comfortable. This is most likely connected with fear. Maybe you are afraid that your new boss might not like what your intuition is telling you or maybe you think that they will just ignore your advice because you are new. Whatever the case may be, you just need to regain your confidence in yourself. You got to where you are now for a reason, it is because you worked hard for it and deserve to be there. The universe believes in your skills and abilities enough to put you in a position where you should be. You have listened to your intuition before and it made you who you are today and it led you to a great path so listen to it and be confident not just on yourself but also be confident on your intuition.

3. Lack Of Trust

Mistakes can happen more often than we want them to. Sometimes we can just make the wrong decisions. No one is perfect and you should not beat yourself up for being imperfect and making a mistake. You may have lost your trust in your own judgement. You made a decision and it turned out to be wrong and now you feel like you can no longer trust your intuition anymore. Being a human being means making mistakes and most of the time, making mistakes can be a way for us to learn something. Making mistakes can help us make better decisions in the future if we learn from them. However, those wrong decisions should not affect your trust in yourself. Take some of that confidence that you have regained and know that you are the right person for the job and trust that your intuition will guide you to the right path. Take that path and apply the lessons you have learned from your past mistakes and take your life and career to new heights.

Dream Interpretation

While many people have been studying dreams for many years, the things that we see while we are sleeping are still incredibly misunderstood and not everyone can interpret the meaning behind them. When we are sleeping, our minds are still very active, creating stories and images that can be very vivid, blurry and momentary, does not make any sense, seemingly show us what the future might bring, absolutely terrifying, totally mundane, or even bring us joy and peace to help us relax and be calm. Symbols and signs are the language of a dream. Dreams are not always meant to be taken literally. The details in your dream are connected to a different aspect of your life that it can symbolize. A symbol can bring a feeling or an idea and often has a much more deeper and profound meaning than any one word can bring upon us the dreamer. However, these symbols can also leave us confused and wondering what they mean and what our dream is all about. Obtaining the ability to interpret your dreams or the dreams of other people is a powerful tool that can help you be the best version of yourself and help you help other people understand more about themselves and their feelings and emotions. While analyzing a dream, you can learn about the person's deep secrets and hidden feelings so make sure that they are comfortable with sharing it to you. Dream interpretation works best if you are using it to yourself because there is no one better than you at interpreting your own dreams because you know exactly what happened and how you felt during your dream and you understand yourself more than anyone. Every detail of your dream, even the smallest element is very important and must be considered when you are trying to analyze and understand your dreams. Each symbol represents a feeling, a memory, a mood or something that is coming from your subconscious. Look closely at the characters, objects, places, animals, emotions, and even colors and numbers that show up in your dreams. Even the most trivial detail can be extremely important.

Types Of Dreams

There are several different types of dreams and many different factors that cause these dreams to happen.

1. Standard Dream

A standard dream may vary from person to person but most standard dreams are predominantly visual, this means that the images that you see in your dreams are at the forefront of your dreams, instead of your other senses like smell, touch, or taste. Even though most of us dream in color, some people have dreams that are entirely black and white even though they are not colorblind. Your feelings, emotions, mood, events in news, pain that you feel, violence, your religion, and almost everything that you come across may all influence what you dream is going to be about. The less stressed you are, the more likely it is that you will have a more pleasant dream and if you are more stressed, you are more likely to dream an unpleasant dream. Our dreams can also be very confusing, very strange, and may seem like it is just a bunch of mess but that is totally normal and it has a meaning that is just not literal.

2. Nightmares

Nightmares are dreams that are disturbing, scary, or spooky. Almost all of us experience nightmares every now and then and there is not always a good reason as to why we are having them. Some potential reason for you having nightmares may include watching a horror movie or reading something scary, not getting enough sleep, eating too much right before you go to sleep and not leaving time for your stomach to digest your food properly, side effects of a medication that you are taking, having a high fever or being ill, and having other sleep disorders such as sleep apnea which makes your breathing repeatedly stops and starts, narcolepsy which makes you overwhelmingly drowsy and makes it difficult for you to stay awake for a long period of time, or nightmare disorder which causes you to have abnormally high amounts of frequent nightmares. People that experience a lot of stress or someone who has a mental health condition like anxiety disorder might experience nightmares that are more frightening than usual. And people with post-traumatic stress disorder or PTSD are reported to have recurring nightmares if it is not treated. Most common themes for nightmares are running away from someone or something that is chasing or hunting you down, someone hurting you or hurting someone else in your dream while you watch, and even death of someone in your dream or even the death of yourself. Some lifestyle changes can help you decrease the frequency of your nightmares if you are having a lot of it. You can try exercising at least three times a week, limiting the amount of caffeine and alcohol that you are consuming, avoiding tranquilizers if you are using them, engaging in relaxation techniques such as meditation and yoga before you go to sleep, and establishing a sleep pattern by going to sleep at the same time every night and waking up at the same time every morning. If your child is having nightmares often, you should encourage them to talk to you about their nightmares. Explain to them that nightmares cannot hurt them, it is not really happening and it is not going to happen. Creating a bedtime routine for your child by having them sleep at the same time each night and waking them up at the same time every morning, teaching your child to relax and do deep breathing exercises, making your child write a dream journal to help them track their dreams, having your child rewrite the ending of their nightmares, asking your child to talk to the characters from their nightmare, giving your child items that will help them be comfortable at night while they sleep such as stuffed animals and blanket, and using a nightlight or leaving their bedroom door open at night while they sleep can also help them deal with their nightmares and may cause them to have less frequent nightmares.

3. Night Terrors

When you are experiencing a night terror, you wake up terrified but you may not remember what you dreamed about or you only have a vague idea of what it is. Most of the time it is the former and you would not remember your dreams from a night terror. In a night terror, you may wake up screaming, sweating, breathing hard, with a racing heart rate, kicking or moving violently and even jumping out of your bed, or very disoriented and not sure where you are or what is going on at the moment. Having a nightmare and a night terror can be very similar and linked to each other but the main difference between them is that night terrors are more common with children because they experience more non-REM sleep while nightmares can affect everyone no matter what their age is. Nightmares are also more vividly recalled dreams most of the time while night terrors are easily forgotten and you would not even remember it as soon as you wake up.

4. Lucid Dreams

Lucid dreams are dreams that are happening while your consciousness is awake and you are aware that you are dreaming but your body is sleeping. You are aware that the events that are happening and flashing through your brain are not really happening at all but the dream feels real and vivid. Sometimes you may even be able to control how your dream will unfold just like you are directing a movie while you are sleeping. This can help you control your dreams when you are having a recurring dream or nightmare. Lucid dreams are happening most often while we are in a period of our sleep called a REM sleep or rapid eye movement sleep. This phase is a period of very deep sleep marked by rapid eye motions, faster breathing, and more brain activity. We usually enter REM sleep about 90 minutes after we fall asleep. At first it lasts for about 10 minutes but as you sleep longer, each REM period is longer than the last one before it and finally lasts for up to an hour.

Lucid dreaming can help us lessen our anxiety. The sense of power and control that you feel during a lucid dream might stay with you even after you wake up and it may make you feel empowered. When we are aware that we are in a dream, you can do whatever we want with the dream's story and its ending. This might serve as a therapy for people who are having nightmares because they can control their dream and get rid of their nightmares by turning it into something more pleasant. Lucid dreams can also help us develop our motor skills. Some studies suggest that it can be possible to improve simple things like tapping your fingers more quickly by practicing it while you are dreaming. The same parts of our brain are activated whether we are imagining the movements while we are awake or even if it is just while we are dreaming. Our problem-solving skills can also be improved while we are lucid dreaming. Lucid dreams can help solve problems that are more about the creative side of our brain like solving a conflict with another person than with a logical problem such as a math question. This means that lucid dreaming can help develop your creativity, it might be easier for you to come up with new and better ideas or insights about something if you are practicing lucid dreaming.

However, lucid dreaming does not only bring positive things, it may also cause problems like having less sleep quality because vivid dreams might wake us up and make it harder for us to get back to sleep afterwards. And you might not be able to sleep well if you are focusing too much on having a lucid dream. Lucid dreaming can also cause confusion, hallucinations, and even delirium to some people who have certain mental health problems, it may blur the lines between what is real and what is just their imagination. This might cause them to not know anymore which is real and which is not real and it might cause them to go crazy in the worst case scenario.

Here are some methods to be able to raise your chance of having a lucid dream:

- Testing Reality – This is the process of pausing at different times of the day to see whether you are dreaming or you are awake. You can try to do something that is not possible to do in the real world just like pushing your finger through your hand or trying to inhale while you have your mouth and nose closed. You can also do something that is usually difficult to do in a dream like reading a page in a book, trying to look at yourself in a mirror, or try to see if you can find your smartphones because even though we spend so much time with our smartphones, you can rarely see it with you in a dream.

- Have a dream journal – Some people reported that they have an easier time having a lucid dream after they have kept a log of all their dreams because they become more focused on their dreams because of it. Writing a dream journal may not help on their own but it will definitely be useful if you combine them with other methods to help you in having a lucid dream.

- Wake up and sleep again immediately – Waking up after you sleep for five hours and staying awake for a brief moment and then going back to sleep again can help you enter REM sleep period more often can help you have lucid dreams because they mostly happen while we are in a REM sleep period.

- Mnemonic induction of having a lucid dream – Mnemonic induction means that after waking up after sleeping for five hours, you are going to tell yourself several times what your next dream is happening, you will know that you are dreaming as soon as you go back to sleep. This triggers your prospective memory, which is the act of remembering to do something in the future, to make yourself experience lucid dreams.

- Taking suitable drugs – Several drugs such as food supplements and medicinal plants may have effects on our sleep and dreams. This can induce lucid dreams but it is not recommended as we are still not sure if it is safe and how well they actually work.

- Using devices that induce lucid dreams – Some masks or headbands that produce lights or sound can make us lucid dreams. You can also use a recording device to record yourself saying that you will remember you are dreaming the next time you do and play that recorded message while you are sleeping.

5. **Daydreams**

All the other types of dreams happen while we are sleeping while daydream is the type of dream that happens while you are awake and not while you are sleeping. Daydreams happen while we are aware of it but you may still feel like you are not fully awake or aware of what is happening around you. If you see someone daydreaming, you may think that they look zoned out or lost in their thoughts. Daydreaming usually involves other people whether real or imagined. Daydreaming about people that you know personally is connected to positive well-being while daydreaming about people that you are not close to can be connected more to loneliness and worse well-being.

Daydreaming can have negative effects on your life if you do it too much. There are times that daydreaming can be productive and useful but if you do it too much, it may cause you to lose your focus and forget important information that you need to know. If you are at your work and you are trying to complete an important task, daydreaming can interfere with your work and cause you to either slow down or stop completely what you are currently doing for a couple of minutes. If your job consists of operating heavy machinery, daydreaming might even be harmful to your health if you continue to let it reduce your focus and concentration. Daydreaming can also be harmful for your mental well-being if you are always having negative thoughts in your daydreams. While most of us daydream about our desires and fantasies, other people might daydream about doing harmful things to other people or even themselves. There have been many cases of people who are suicidal that are driving along the road and daydreaming about crashing into something. Sometimes, these kinds of daydreaming fantasies can be rather involved with a great amount of detail. It is almost like it is an actual plan rather than being just a fantasy. When it involves something that could cause harm to you or to other people, daydreaming is most likely going to be a detrimental thing for you.

On the other hand, you can also use daydreaming to your advantage. One way you can do this is to set aside a time every day for daydreaming. Even though we mostly daydream spontaneously, you can still set a particular time when you sit in a quiet place and begin to start daydreaming. Many people find this to be an ideal exercise to relieve their stress after a long and hard day at work. This can also help relieve your stress after having a major argument with your friend, family members or even after a traumatic life event.

Daydreaming allows your mind to wander around and forget everything that is bothering you for a short period of time. This practice alone can help you keep your sanity when you are going through tough times. By allowing yourself to escape from a stressful situation even temporarily, you can return to that same situation with a new attitude and possibly even a solution to the problem that is causing the stress that you are experiencing.

Furthermore, daydreaming is not just a way to relieve stress, it can also be a way that many people choose to be able to relax their mind. Daydreaming allows your mind to take a break for the duration of the entire time that you allocate to let your mind wander around. Since you are letting your mind take a break, you can often return from a daydreaming session with a mind that is refreshed and feels renewed. Most of the time, this is all we need to go back to a task that we are currently stuck with and be able to finish it. Because most of the time, working on the same task for a long period of time can cause your mind to get bored and stop concentrating on it. Daydreaming can relieve your mind from the pressure and stress that is coming from the issue that you are facing for a couple of minutes and as a result, you will return feeling refreshed and ready to complete the task. Daydreaming can also help us manage conflict.

Other people might choose to use daydreaming as a way to manage the conflict that they are facing. This is often known as organized daydreaming and it involves imagining the different ways to deal with the conflict that they are facing or conflicts that may arise in the future. Using this method of daydreaming can help you review specific situations in your mind so that you can be prepared for a variety of things. For example, you may often daydream about what would happen and what would you do if somebody tried to rob you on the street. By using organized daydreaming, you can visualize a couple of different possible scenarios so that you can be better prepared in case it happens as long as what you visualize is within the realm of possibilities and not just fantasizing about having super powers.

Daydreaming can also help us maintain the relationships that we currently have. When couples or friends are away from each other, daydreaming about spending time with the other person can often make you feel like you are still together with them. You can either daydream about the times that you have spent together in the past with your friend or your romantic partner, or you can daydream about what you would do together in a certain situation. For example, if your close friend moved far away from the city that you are currently living in, you can daydream about how it might turn out if you were with him when you got a new job that you always wanted. While daydreaming can never be the same as actually being with those special people in your life, it can help you remember them fondly and keep you thinking about them rather than letting them slip out of your mind and maybe even forgetting them at some point.

Daydreaming can also be used as an effective method to help you boost your productivity. If you allow yourself a couple of minutes in the middle of the day to daydream about a problem that you have at work or in any other situation, your mind may think about a variety of ways to solve that problem that you are having. It can also uplift your mood and it will make you feel better overall. When you feel good, the more likely it is that you are going to be productive, unlike when you are not feeling good you become tired and you do not want to do anything. As a result, daydreaming can make us more motivated to do our job or a task that is assigned to us and move on to the next thing we need to do.

Because daydreaming helps us to be more motivated and boosts our productivity, it can help us achieve our goals as well. If you can daydream about being successful at a certain job or even in a certain point of your life, you are more likely to reach the goals that you are aiming for. Most of the time, visualization is an important key to striving towards a goal that you have. It is a common technique used by high performing professionals such as athletes and other people whom society would consider successful. Therefore, this can also work for everyone and yourself.

Daydreaming can also help you concentrate and focus on a higher goal for yourself. The more that we think about our ultimate goal and focus on the steps we can do to achieve that goal, the more likely it is that we will be able to reach that goal. We might even be able to achieve our goal faster if we are using daydreaming efficiently and not overdoing it. Although daydreaming is mostly seen as just spacing out and doing nothing, we can use it to our advantage because it not only boosts our creativity and problem-solving skills, but it can also help us concentrate more and focus on a specific task. It helps our mind wander to thoughts and areas that it might not wander if you had not set aside a time to daydream. If you are using it efficiently and effectively, daydreaming can be one of the most powerful techniques that you can use to reach your ultimate goal.

6. Recurring Dreams

Recurring dreams are dreams that you experience which repeat more than once. Most of the time, they have themes that are related to being chased, confrontations, or falling. You can either have neutral recurring dreams or recurring nightmares. If you have recurring nightmares, it may be connected to an underlying mental health condition, substance abuse, or a certain medication that you are taking. Your dreams do not have to be completely identical each time for it to be considered as a recurring dream. For instance, you may be having a dream about driving on a bridge and suddenly that bridge starts to collapse. If you dream again about driving on a different car on a different bridge but the bridge still collapsed it would still count as a recurring dream even if some of the details are not completely the same. Since recurring dreams can sometimes begin in your childhood, they might change a little bit over time to reflect the changing experiences that you are having and your changing view of the world.

It is believed that recurring dreams can generally reflect important things in our life such as unmet needs, things that frustrates us or issues from the past that we have not addressed yet. For example, you have probably had a dream that is about forgetting a final exam or not being able to submit your research paper on time. Even though this dream is from a stress that you have experienced while you are a student, it can easily come up again later in your life even after you have graduated a long time ago. Since this dream is related to your desire to succeed and your worries about failing at something, you may have this kind of dream anytime you are faced with an event that causes you to have similar feelings. This could be an event like a job interview, a research proposal, or a big date with someone you really like. If you had a bad dream and it upsets you the first time you have had it, having the same dreams multiple times probably would feel much worse and would not make you feel any better. We cannot always directly control the contents of our dreams, but it is possible to take more indirect action by trying to resolve the problem that is causing the stress in your life which causes the bad dream to happen. No matter what kinds of challenges you may be facing right now, a therapist can offer you guidance on taking care of yourself and managing stress productively if you think that you need professional help and cannot do these things on your own. In therapy, you will be able to identify and explore the causes of the unwanted feelings and emotions that you are having, address their effect on your life, and learn helpful techniques of coping with the anxiety and stress that you are dealing with. Although it is generally not possible to get rid of all the stress that you are feeling, changing the way you respond to it can help lower any associated frustration and can lead to improvements in your mood, outlook of your life, and in your dreams.

7. False Awakenings

False awakenings are a type of dream where a person may think that he has already woken up but in reality, they are actually still sleeping and have not woken up yet. If you have ever found yourself dreaming that you woke up, but it was actually still a part of your dream then that is a false awakening. Some people may even experience nested dreams where there is more than one false awakening happening in the same dream. False awakenings can be related to having sleep disorders such as insomnia or sleep apnea, anticipation of waking up or knowing that you need to wake up early for a certain reason, or the noises and other things that disturbs and interrupts your sleep without fully waking you up. Stress and anxiety in our daily life can also have an impact on our sleep quality and may potentially appear in our dreams. If you are worried about something that is going to happen shortly after you have woken up, you might dream about waking up and getting ready to face the stressful event that is bothering you. These stressful events may include an upcoming difficult exam or a job interview for a job that you really want to get. Even though it might feel strange, false awakenings generally do not pose any cause for medical concern. There is no evidence that suggests that false awakening occurs as a symptom of any physical or mental health condition. However, it is still worth looking into any unusual occurrence that is regularly disrupting your sleep. False awakening can happen alongside other symptoms that do have a more serious case. Talk to a healthcare professional or a sleep specialist if you also notice other symptoms like having trouble going to sleep or staying asleep, feel fatigue or extreme exhaustion after several hours in bed, severe sleepiness during the day, or frequent nightmares. Improving the sleep that you are getting each night can help reduce the frequency of false awakenings. Turning off your phone and any other electronics you have at least one hour before you go to sleep, using a sleep calculator and figuring out how much sleep you really need, and taking some time to wind down and relax before going to bed can help improve the quality of your sleep to reduce the frequency of your false awakenings. Mental health concerns like depression and anxiety can also contribute to the disturbing dreams that you are having and may affect the quality of your sleep. It is a good idea to reach out to a therapist for any mental health symptoms that do not go away after a week or two, especially if your mood change is also occurring with the physical health symptoms such as change in your sleeping habits.

8. Healing Dreams

Healing dreams are the type of dreams that have been described as dreams that can bring balance or harmony to your mind and body, give you a sense of connection, purpose, or meaning, bring about reconciliation, and leave you feeling joyful or at peace. This is when you dream about a happy dream and it makes you feel good even after waking up. This may happen with the help of your spirit guide. If your spirit guide feels like you need something to make you feel better, they can show you a pleasant imagery in your dream and make it a healing dream. You can also ask them yourself to help you have a healing dream. If you have a strong connection with your spirit guide and you communicate often, you can ask them favors to help you in your daily life and asking for healing dreams is one of them. Our spirit guide is there to help guide us and support us so it is likely for them to grant your request. Healing dreams can also occur after you have dealt with a major conflict that is bothering you for a long time. Because you feel like there is a huge weight that is taken off your shoulder, you can relax more and have a better quality sleep which can also induce a healing dream and you will feel more happiness as soon as you wake up.

9. **Prophetic Dreams**

Prophetic dreams are dreams that we psychic have that foretold a future event that is yet to happen. If you dream of something happening and then it happens later, it means that you have had a prophetic dream. You may experience déjà vu from already having seen the event that happened in your dream. Dreams are considered an important way to impart wisdom from the universe to us psychic empaths and it can even predict the future. Some people believe that a prophetic dream is just our subconscious trying to predict a certain scenario and having you dream about it to prepare. But in reality, prophetic dreams come from the spiritual world and it is sent to you to help you manage the situation and act accordingly. This kind of dream could be a message sent to you by your spirit guide to warn you about upcoming dangers to help you avoid it or to help other people be saved by your help. Prophetic dreams are not just about future events, it could also be about current events that are happening but you are not aware of. It is a message sent to you by the universe to help you deal with that current scenario or to alert you that you need to do something about it. For example, if you dream about your friend abusing drugs to help them deal with a problem they are currently facing. That dream can either be happening right now or is going to happen in the future. It is sent to you so that you can help your friend and bring him back to the correct path. Try talking to your friend and help him deal with his problems so that he would not need to turn to abusing drugs just to escape the reality of the problem he is facing. Prophetic dreams are sent to you not only to help you save yourself but to also help you help other people save themselves from straying away from the right path.

10. Vivid Dreams

Vivid dreams are almost always connected with waking up during a REM sleep, this is the period of your sleep when your dreams are most vivid and are more easily remembered because of the increase in our brain's activity. While we can consider all the dreams that we experience while in a REM sleep period vivid, vivid dreams is a particularly intense dream that feels very real and gives us a strong feeling associated with it even after waking up. It is also very easy to remember a vivid dream more than a usual dream because of the intense feeling that came with the vivid dream. Vivid dreams can be caused by sleep disorders that cause a lack of sleep such as narcolepsy or insomnia. Changes to your sleep schedule such as when you are flying overseas and going to sleep at a different time or getting less sleep than usual can also increase the chance of experiencing vivid dreams.

Usually, vivid dreams are not something that we need to be concerned about but sometimes they may affect us during a certain part of our lives. Negative vivid dreams, especially if they are happening for a long period of time such as a couple of weeks to even a month can be emotionally disturbing, can disrupt your sleep and lower the quality of your sleep. And that can cause both mental and physical health problems. A common side effect of vivid dreams includes daytime sleepiness which can cause you to lose concentration and focus. It can also cause memory problems that can affect your productivity while you are at work or at school. It can even affect your ability to carry our regular daily tasks such as taking a shower or driving. Even the smallest task can become dangerous if you get distracted and you are not focusing on doing it. Vivid dreams can also be emotionally draining because of the intense emotions that it brings which can cause depression and anxiety symptoms. This can be a very concerning problem especially if your vivid dreams persist over a long period of time. You may also find yourself consciously or subconsciously avoiding going to bed or falling asleep because you fear that you will have another negative vivid dream.

Common Dreams And Their Meaning

1. Dreams About Flying

Many of us have already experienced having a dream where we are flying. This kind of dream can be very exciting and might even be liberating for some of us but they can sometimes be frightening especially if you are afraid of heights. Dreams about flying usually represent two different sides, it can represent feelings of freedom and independence while on the other hand, this dream can also indicate a desire to run away or escape from the realities of our daily lives. We often dream about flying alone which shows that we are independent, but because it involves positive feelings of pleasure most of the time, flying can also portray our sexuality, especially the parts of it that are expressing freedom from social restraints and social norms. Dream about flying is a sign that you have freed yourself from something difficult or frustrating. Something that has been weighing you down in your life and it is because you managed to make a decision or you rise above the restrictions of a heavy responsibility. If you feel scared in your dream while you are flying or you see an obstacle that is in front of you preventing you from going forward, that may mean that you feel that there is something holding you back or preventing you from doing something that you want to do. It is the feeling that something is almost about to take off but it is not quite there yet. It could be a relationship or a job that you want. Pay attention to the details in your dream and try to figure out what it represents in your life and that will really show your feelings and emotions on a deeper level.

2. Dreams About Being Naked In Public

Have you ever had one of those embarrassing dreams where you are in a public place such as your workplace or in school and you are wearing absolutely nothing? And you feel great relief as soon as you realize that you are just dreaming. Do not worry because these kinds of dreams are also common and not unusual. Dreaming about yourself being naked can mean that you are feeling vulnerable and exposed. You feel like you are not being true to yourself or you are afraid that your imperfections and shortcomings might be revealed. It may be time for you to find a way to get yourself to be comfortable at opening yourself up to other people. However, if you do not feel any shame while you are naked in public, this might mean that you want to be acknowledged and admired for who you are and what you are doing in your life. You want to have more exposure.

3. Dreams About Snakes

Snakes in our dreams most often represent a toxic person or situation in our life and depending on the other details in our dreams, a snake in our dream can mean different things. If you felt afraid after seeing the snake, it is likely that you are feeling fear about a person or situation in your life and you need to be wary about them. If you are bit by the snake in your dream, it means that you need physical healing and the bite represents a need for an antidote to help you fight the venom of the snake. The area of your body that the snake bit can be a sign of where you need to be healed. If the snake climbs your body, it might be giving you a sign that you have an imbalance in that particular area of your body. If you are seeing the same snake over and over in your different dreams this means that you are overwhelmed by the toxic person or situation that is always present in your life. It could be a toxic spouse or a colleague that is always bothering you. The more that you see the same snake in your dream, the more present that person or situation is in your current life. Even the breed of the snake that you have seen in your dream also has a significant meaning. If you see a rattlesnake in your dream, it could represent a warning or a red flag caused by a situation that has already happened with a particular person or situation. If you see a garter snake, it indicates that a situation that seems threatening has already passed and that situation is not going to cause you any harm. The garter snake is not a venomous breed of snake so it represents someone that we were wary of at first but later you will realize that this person is not going to harm you. The place where you saw the snake in your dream also represents a certain meaning, if you see a snake in your bedroom, it means that it could be related to someone or something that is close and intimate with you. If you see the snake at work, it could mean that a situation or a person at work is not making you feel comfortable.

4. Dreams About A Cheating Partner

Dreaming that your significant other or your romantic partner is cheating on you with somebody else can be really distressing. In some cases, other people even start to wonder if their partner is really cheating on them and the dream that they had is true. Does dreaming about your partner cheating on you means that it might happen or that it is already happening? While in some cases, this kind of dream might be a sign that you fear that your partner is cheating on you, but most of the time, this does not mean that your partner is cheating on you or will cheat on you in the future. Dreams about your partner cheating is just a sign that one of you is not getting what you need or want from the relationship that you have right now. This can be a sign that you need to talk about your relationship and give each other a chance to talk about something that you might feel lacking in your relationship. As long as you do not wake up pissed off at your partner for something that they did not really do in real life and just in your dreams. It is letting you know that you need to correct something in your relationship. You and your partner can spend more time together like having date nights, watching movies together, or even as simple as eating dinner together, whatever it may be as long as you are both happy. One more meaning to this kind of dream could be coming from a broader range of feelings about wanting to escape or try something different, it is not just all about your relationship with your partner. It could also be an issue with the relationship you have with yourself. You may have thoughts about quitting your job and living a simpler life in a remote farm and that desire is growing in you and you want to actually do it but you just cannot bring yourself to do it. Or this kind of dream could simply represent the idea of going into a new personal project or exploring something new that relates to intellectual things such as learning a new skill.

5. **Dreams About Falling**

Dreams about you falling from a high place are very common and almost everyone has experienced it at one point in their life. There is a popular misconception that if you hit the ground while you are falling in your dream you will die in real life, but that is just simply not true. So, what exactly does that dream about you falling truly means? Well, according to many popular dream interpretations, dreams about falling are a sign that your life is not going well. It might be telling you that you need to rethink some of your life choices or consider a direction in some parts of your life. It can also be associated with the feeling of being overwhelmed and out of control or you may be feeling unsupported and insecure. And the falling in your dreams is telling you that you are hanging too tightly to a certain situation in your life and you need to relax, let yourself go more often and enjoy your life more.

6. Dreams About Being Chased

If you are being chased by something or someone in your dream, this can be really scary for you while you are in your dream. This means that there is an issue in your life that you want to face but you do not know how to confront it. You are trying to avoid something in your life and it could either be a desire to escape from your own desires or fears. The key to figuring out what this kind of dream might mean depends a bit on identifying what kind of pursuer you have. If you are being chased by a monster, that monster may be a manifestation of an addiction, an indiscretion, or a debt that you currently have and is bothering you maybe even unconsciously. If you are being chased by an animal, this might mean that you are hiding from anger, passion, or any other feelings and emotions that you have that you want to suppress. If the one that is chasing you is a mysterious shadow or an unknown figure, this might represent a childhood experience or past trauma that you are dealing with. If the one that is chasing you is someone of your opposite sex, it might suggest that you are afraid of love or you are being haunted by your past relationship. If it is someone that you know personally, your associations about that person who is chasing you in your dream are often more insightful than focusing on the actual person that is chasing you. Take note that other people in our dreams can be a substitution for other people or even a substitution for a part of yourself. This dream about you being chased might be a sign that is trying to tell you that it is time to face all your fears and pursue something that you have been putting aside for some time.

7. **Dreams About Losing Teeth**

Dreaming about losing teeth can have multiple meanings and can suggest many things even though it is a very common dream. It can mean that you are worried about your physical appearance or your attractiveness. It may also mean that you are concerned about your ability to talk to other people or you are concerned that you may have said something embarrassing to someone. Dreams about losing your teeth could also be your pent up anxiety manifesting itself in the form of a dream. You may think of this as being worried about not realizing your own potential, you being not competent enough, or lacking the needed strength or power for you to take on the world. You may experience these kinds of dreams when something big happens in your life such as you losing a job and you may have lost your feeling of being in control with your job that you lost. Our teeth symbolize how confident, powerful, and in control we feel like really are. And in the dream of losing your teeth, it means that you are losing your personal power, your confidence and your ability to be in control, be assertive, and be decisive. It is a common dream when you are in times of change and transition.

8. Dreams About Dying

Another common subject of a dream is death and this one can be particularly concerning. You can sometimes dream of the death of someone close to you such as a close friend or one of your family members, or sometimes you may also dream of even dying yourself. Just like death, change can also be very scary because we usually do not know what is on the other side of the change that is going to happen which is why death in a dream can mean that you are feeling that something is coming to an end in your life and something is about to change.

A dream about the death of someone close to us can reflect a similar fear of change, especially if it is related to your kids reaching a certain milestone in their life and growing up. This change can indicate that a child is growing up and the parent's mind begins to worry about where the younger version of the kid went. This dream about dying can reflect a sort of mourning phase for the inevitable passage of time.

Your reaction to the death in your dream is also an important detail to pay attention to. If you are calm and peaceful about the death in your dream, it could mean that you have something in your life that you are ready to let go of. However, if you are scared and panicking in your dream about death, then you are most likely not quite ready yet and you feel uncomfortable letting things go.

9. Dreams About Taking A Test

Dreams about taking a test could mean that you have an underlying fear of failure and making mistakes. This dream is usually connected to our work because it is said that our first job ever is being a student in our school. Dreaming about taking a test is common when you are facing a work challenge. If you feel like you are well prepared while taking the test then it would mean that you are confident about the work challenge that you are facing and you feel like you can succeed in it if you give it your best shot. Examinations are a stressful experience for us because we are made to face up to our shortcomings. If you dream about failing an exam, being late to it, or coming unprepared can mean that you also feel unprepared for the challenge that you are currently facing in your life. However, you can use this fear of failure and making mistakes to your advantage. Use it as your fuel to drive yourself to work even harder and strive to correctly do the things you need to do. Our fear of being unprepared can be the inspiration we need to actually drive us to being totally ready to do the things we need to do.

10. Dreams About An Empty Room

Dreaming about an empty room might imply that you have got hidden talents that you are not making use of because you might also not know about it. The more that you spend time exploring what talents you might have that you are not aware about, it is more likely that you will find more opportunities for yourself along the way.

However, if that empty room is accompanied by a feeling of discomfort or fear while you are in the room, then it might represent something very different. If your dream is about going into an empty room and it feels spooky or scary, that can mean that you have realized something about yourself that is unexpected in the past one to three days. It can also be something old that you have not paid attention to before. It could be any part of your life such as your job or a relationship with your friend or a family member that you have shut the door on. You should try opening that door even if you are scared and for you to face your fear.

CHAPTER 4: DEVELOP YOUR EMPATHIC ABILITIES TO FIND THE RIGHT WORK

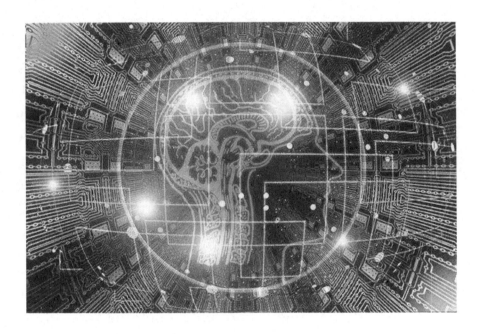

The Ways Of Developing Yourself As An Empath

Embrace Your Creativity

No matter what line of work you are in, making use of your creativity can really benefit you. Using your creativity can help you with solving problems, communicating with someone and a number of other things in any kind of job. Creativity is also important to our personal life. It can be very liberating and it can bring you a lot of happiness when you start to embrace your creativity.

Here are a couple of things to do to help you embrace your creativity:

- Experiment – There are so many things available for us to express our creativity so do not feel tied down to any one particular method. Be open to trying out new things. You may be surprised at how easily your creativity opens up when you find the thing that clicks with you and helps you express your creativity.

- Do not be scared – Fear is the number one reason why people do not try out new things. They are afraid of failing, they are worried about how they will look and how it will affect them. What you need to understand is that embracing your creativity does not need to be for anyone but yourself. Do not be afraid of what others will say, if you fail you just need to learn from your mistakes and try again.

- Find something you can be passionate about – Without passion, creativity is hard to initiate, but when you can find a thing that you love, you will be overflowing with creativity. Take some time to think about what your passions are. What is it that you like doing very much? Hone in on those things that you love to do and start thinking about what you love about it so much and your creativity will surely start to kick in.

- Be spontaneous – Do not overthink things and just go with whatever it is that just feels right for you. If you think about things too much, you may start to have doubts and may start to play it safe. It may be hard to just let yourself do something creative but there is nothing wrong with just allowing yourself to do whatever you want and see what will come out of it.

- Always carry a notepad – Inspiration plays a big part in our creativity. We never know when inspiration is going to hit us and it will not wait for us until we are ready for it to happen. We need to be always ready anytime for when inspiration is going to hit us. That is why you should always carry a notepad with you. Write down every idea that pops into your head whenever you get them because you might forget them later on if you do not write it down right away. It is not always going to be great but the ability to go through every idea that comes to your mind is a valuable ability to have for your creative process.

Turn Your Home Into Protective Heaven And Organized Home

Turning your home into a protective heaven and organized home means that you will be cleaning your house and organizing it so that it is filled with positive energy that can help you relax and get rid of all the negative energies that you absorbed from other people. Getting rid of the clutter in your house and organizing your furniture and appliances can make you feel calm because a house filled with clutter can be overwhelming and it produces negative energies which can make you feel tired and drained. Setting up a garden or even placing a couple of plants inside or outside your house also help contribute to improving the overall quality of the positive energy that is coming from your house. It is also a great decoration to make your house look livelier. Having a home where you can relax is very important for a psychic empath because this is where you will spend most of your time processing the energy that you absorbed outside. If you have absorbed plenty of negative energy outside and when you get home your house is filled with clutter and you cannot relax then it will cause more stress for you and it may be harmful to your well-being. That is why it is important to keep our house clean and well organized.

Make New Friends

Making new friends is important for a psychic empath because having good friends is good for our well-being. They can help us offset the negative energies that are around us if you have a friend that is filled with positivity. Friends also improves our self-esteem and reduces stress by being there for us to support us in times of need and offers us companionship. To make new friends, you need to be kind and pay attention to the other person and listen to them. After you let them share details about themselves, you should also open up and share your feelings with them. This builds intimacy with the other person and brings you closer to each other. Making yourself available to them and showing that you can be trusted is also important to nurture your friendship. Being dependable and reliable is something that can make the other people feel more comfortable around you. Making an effort to see them regularly and checking up on them in between meet-ups is also a good idea.

Do not be afraid to attend community events to meet up with other people. Of course, you will not be friends with everyone that you meet, but if you maintain a friendly attitude, it can help you improve the chances of meeting a new friend. Just be sure to manage your time properly around crowds so that you would not be overwhelmed with their energies. Give yourself some time to relax and recover after being with a crowd.

The Desire to Eat Healthier Food

Having the desire to eat healthier food will translate to having a healthier body. If we have a healthy body, it will be easier for our mind to relax and do what it needs to do instead of worrying about what is happening with our body. Eating healthy food is not just for our body, it also improves our memory and brain health which gives us a better mood and higher energy level. This is important for us psychic empaths because we are constantly bombarded with negative energies and this could be extremely overwhelming for us. Having a healthy body and a healthy mind can help us process these negative energies more easily and we will have an easier time dealing with the pressure of our psychic abilities.

The Sensation Of Pressure Disappears

Once you have accepted the fact that you cannot change everything in your life and you just have to live with it, the pressure that you experience will disappear. It is not an easy task to do but accepting that there are some things that happen in our daily life that we cannot do anything about will help you focus your time and energy on the things that you can affect such as how you can react to the situation instead of trying to change the situation that you cannot control. It is true that there are some scenarios in our life that we can control but there are also some of them that we cannot. That is why it is important to learn how to adapt to your current situation. Like our ability to absorb other people's negative emotions, we cannot stop ourselves from sensing and absorbing them but we can change our reaction to it. If you learn to accept these emotions and process it properly, it will be a strong tool that you can use to your advantage instead of being a problem that is weighing you down.

Connection With The Spirits

Having connection with the spirit world grants a psychic empath great gifts that they can use to help themselves or to help other people. Knowing your spirit guide and connecting with them can help you be guided on what you need to do with your life. Since spirit guides are a being that only wants to help us and guide us, it is alright to surrender ourselves to them and follow their guidelines. They also help us improve our psychic abilities by helping us visualize things by sending us imagery through our mind's eyes. Communicating with your spirit guide regularly while you are meditating is a good practice that will help you improve not only your psychic abilities but also the quality of your life. Spirit guides are filled with positive energies and will also make us feel positive and energized after connecting with them.

Heightened Sensitivity of your Physical Senses

Their intuition is not just the only thing that a psychic empath uses, they also use their physical senses to help them figure out things with higher success. Their sense of hearing and touch is also sensitive and can be used to detect energies within their surroundings. A psychic empath can hear a message sent to them by the universe to guide them on what they need to do and how they should approach a certain situation. Being able to sense the emotions and feelings of other people can also help them develop their sense of sight so that they can find the source of that energy and help them or try to avoid them if necessary.

Common Myths That Psychic Empaths Should Never Believe

Even though empaths have wonderful gifts that are often greatly appreciated by those who are around them, some people may often have misguided perceptions towards them. Many beliefs about empaths are entirely opposite to what the truth is. It may be possible that an empath is branded as being overly sentimental or dramatic. Understanding the common misconceptions about empaths is the first step to teaching everyone around and getting rid of these misunderstandings.

Empaths Are Self-Absorbed And Only Cares About Themselves

It is true that empaths are unexplainably moody and quiet on the outside most of the time but this is not because they are extremely absorbed into thinking too much about themselves and their own feelings. To be precise, a psychic empath is often deeply affected by the feelings and emotions coming from other people that they absorb and experience as his own. An empath's ability to intuitively feel the feelings of other people can sometimes weigh him down so much. In reality, it is one of the characteristics of a psychic empath to pay more attention to the needs of other people than his own needs. They often focus more on other people rather than focusing on themselves.

Empaths Have Mental Health Problems

Empaths are prone to absorbing negative energies from their surroundings and this creates a psychological disturbance within them most of the time but this does not mean that they are mentally ill. Empaths are great listeners, counselors, and people to share a secret with and because of these reasons it is more common for other people to be drawn towards an empath because of their sincere and caring nature.

That is why empaths can experience a lot of emotional baggage being shared to them by other people most of the time, and they may have a harder time releasing themselves from the negative energy that can linger in their mind and body afterwards. Unfortunately, this can cause a lot of depressive emotions to stay with the psychic empath. As a result, they can appear to be mentally ill or depressed and, in some cases, they can sometimes even be legitimately ill. However, most of the time, the empath is congested with the remains of the harmful emotional energy. The root of the problem is not the psychic empath and it is just the result of the negative emotional energy that they absorb around them.

Empaths Are Weak Psychologically

Empaths are highly sensitive and in harmony with their surrounding environment but they are not psychologically weak. Empaths are always accumulating the feelings, emotions, and energy of other people and this may result in a plenty of inner emotional tension for the empath. That is why they are prone to crying or showing signs of being psychologically weak. In addition to that, empaths also usually find it very hard to partake in many normal activities. For example, watching a documentary about the suffering of other people can be very emotionally upsetting for a psychic empath and getting a job in a place that has plenty of people can be overwhelming and tiring for an empath because they will be constantly bombarded by other people's feelings and emotions. Therefore, it is not surprising that an empath is often perceived as psychologically weak to a person that does not understand the constant pressure of being a psychic empath. The fact that most empaths are not driven clinically insane by the amount of emotional flow that they are experiencing is proof that psychic empaths have a strong mental strength.

Empaths Are Lazy

Empaths may often lack emotional, mental, or physical energy because of their ability to sense other people's emotions but this does not mean that we are lazy. CFS or Chronic Fatigue Syndrome have been commonly linked to psychic empaths. When our mind is always overloaded with stress, pressure, or tension, that also translates to our body and drains our energy. This can often result in sickness such as the CFS mentioned earlier, headaches, insomnia or fibromyalgia which is a widespread pain across our bones and muscles accompanied by fatigue, memory, mood, and sleep issues. So, most of the time, empaths lack the energy to do many things and just prefer to relax and take a rest instead.

Empaths Can Stop Being An Empath

If you are a psychic empath, you will not be able to stop absorbing energy no matter how hard you try. Empaths have a hypersensitive nervous system that can sense the energy that is around them. It is not possible to stop sensing these energies. If you try to deny or reject the energies around you, all the energies that you resist will just build up in your energy field and it will cause you more pain. It is important for a psychic empath to awaken their psychic abilities and embrace their gifts so that their own energy and other people's energy can flow freely and not cause any further inconvenience.

Empaths All Have History Of Trauma

Other people say that the only way for a person to be emotionally sensitive and become a psychic empath is if they have experienced a childhood trauma. It is a common misconception that if someone is responsive to other people's feelings and emotions, they are also coming from a place of extreme pain. It is true that there may be some empaths who have experienced childhood trauma but it is not correct to believe that the trauma is the force that turned them into an empath. All of us are born with the potential to be highly responsive. What happens to them when we get older is a completely different story altogether.

All Empaths Are Introverted

Some empaths can be introverted but others are also very outgoing. All empaths are not the same and have different personalities. Empaths come in all shapes and sizes, some of them can be introverts, some are extroverts, and others are ambiverts. It is just that introverted empaths are more common than extroverted empaths. An extroverted empath can have difficulties with balancing the time that they need to engage with other people and the time that they need to avoid being distracted by other people. If you are an empath and you have an extroverted personality, you may want to limit the time that you spend with other people so that you will not tire yourself too much. Make sure that you take enough time to relax and process the negative emotional energy from your body after spending time in a crowd.

Empaths Are More Prone To Having An Emotional Outbursts

Empaths are not prone to having an emotional outburst because being subjected to different levels of emotional energy helps them gain emotional control. People who think that empaths are emotionally weak are only basing their claims on an empath's frequent exposure to different energies which can conflict their emotional stability. It is true that empaths may be prone to being moody but that does not mean that they will be aggressive every time that they are provoked. When empaths are processing the emotional energy that they have absorbed from their surroundings, they are going to be moody most of the time. But this does not mean that they are a volatile person who is getting carried away by their emotions. An empath is very stable when it comes to their own emotions. In fact, by learning how to process and control the forces that may affect them, an empath can quickly learn to be calm and relaxed.

CONCLUSION

Being a psychic empath can either be a gift or a curse depending on how you will manage your psychic abilities. If you do not know how to process the negative emotions that you absorb from other people in your day to day life, then it will surely bring you nothing but pain and suffering. This will make it harder for you to be with other people and you will always be agitated. It will be hard for you to remain calm and relaxed.

However, after reading this book, you have learned how to deal with the things that a psychic empath may come across so that you can turn your psychic ability into a powerful tool that can help you be a stronger and better version of yourself instead of being a burden. Learning how to process the emotions of other people and yourself will make you emotionally strong. And learning how to interpret your dreams will make you understand yourself and your situation even better. Because of that, you will be able to learn how to deal with hard situations and how to come out on top.

Now that you have learned more about psychic empaths, how will you use this knowledge to your advantage? Ask yourself how these situations relate to you and what you can do in those situations. Understanding your gift and yourself better is the key to living your life to its greatest potential. Take all the negativities in your life and turn them into something positive.

I know that you have the ability to do that and you will be successful. Trust me and also trust yourself that you can do anything as long as you put your mind into it. The spirit world is there to guide us and support us so do not worry about everything too much and focus on the things that actually matter.

Made in United States
North Haven, CT
05 February 2022

15612352R00108